Shilbottle
its past and its people

Barry Stewart

Shilbottle Colliery Officials (c) 1890
Back row left to right: William Jeffrey (Engineer), Robert Air (Keeker), R.G. Weightman (Rolleyway Man), William Forrest (Deputy), George Young (Fore-overman), James Riddle (Manager).
Front row left to right: ? Elliott (Joiner), ? Bell (Deputy), ? Wilson (Deputy), ? Storey, (Surveying Apprentice), Thomas Waddell (Deputy), ? Storey, Under Manager.

Reproduced with permission of Northumberland Archives NRO 1426-02

Stenlake Publishing

© 2021 Barry Stewart
First Published in the United Kingdom, 2021
Stenlake Publishing Limited
54-58 Mill Square, Catrine, KA5 6RD
www.stenlake.co.uk

ISBN 978-1-84033-903-1

Acknowledgements

Grateful thanks are due to the following people for their advice, stories, photographs and records – allowing them to be used in this book:

Paul Andrucci, Anne Armstrong, David Baillee, Ann Baston, David Brewis, Michael and Richard Brewis, Thomas Carr, Kay Coulson, George Darling, David Dunn, Jacqueline Foster, John Robert Gay, Rev Canon Colin Gough, Peter Egdell, Elisabeth Haddow, Roger Harrison, Jean Hall, Tom Heavyside, Carol Hope, Arthur Hossain, Billy Hossain, Lilian Hume, Phil Huntley, Roy Inglis, Norman Jackson, Susan Armstron Kirkland, Graham Knox, Ronnie Knox, Roy Lambeth (Durham Mining Museum), Paul Letherland, Christopher Lendrum, Judith Line, Brian and Rosemary Lough, Vera Mallon, Irene Marshall, Billy and Sandra McKnight, Ken Middlemist, Joe Nicholson, Gordon Proctor, Raymond Straker, Rev Pat Rennison, Sadie Rennison, Sheila Robertson, John Ryan, Mark Ryder, Tommy Scott, Margery Slater, Sandra Stewart, Paul Ternent (Assistant Archivist, Northumberland Collections, Woodhorn), Alan Tate, Julia Tweedy, Terry Wayman, Margaret Weaver, Kenneth Willcox, Sylvia Willcox, Keith Wilson, Alistair and Maureen Winn, Pamela Vardy, David Young.

Further Reading

Brewis, Henry, *A stroll in the Country*, (Newcastle, Powdene Publicity Ltd) 1999.
Bulmer, T.F. *History and Directory of Northumberland, Tyneside, Wansbeck & Berwick Division*, (Beavis, Stewart and Co, Newcastle upon Tyne) 1887.
Castledine, Malcolm, *Railway Bylines*, (Clophill, Bedfordshire, Irwell Press Ltd.,) May 1999, p.268.
Hedley, Margaret, *Women of the Durham Coalfields in the 19th century*, (History Press, Stroud, Gloucestershire, 2019)
Hodgson, John Crawford, FSA, *History of Northumberland Vol V p 473* (Newcastle upon Tyne, Andrew Reid & Co Ltd) 1899
Jermy, Roger, *Northern Northumberland's Minor Railways, Vol 2, Colliery & Associated Lines*, (Usk, The Oakwood Press, 2011) p. 37
Kelly's Trade Directory for 1861.
Memories of Shilbottle, Millennium Edition p.56
Northumberland County Council, *Plessey, The Story of a Northumberland Woodland* (Hexham, N.C.C., 1984) p.12.
Muckle, William, *No Regrets*, (Newcastle, People's Publications, 1981), p.19
Parson and White Trade Directory for 1827
'Stewart, Barry; *Bilton Banks- The Pit and its People*, Stenlake Publishing, Ayrshire, 2012 pp 4-44.
Stewart, John, *The Life and Times of John Stewart, (an unpublished memoire)* 1995.
Wilson, F.R., 'An Architectural Survey of the Churches in the Archdeaconry of Lindisfarne', (Newcastle, Rivingtons, 1870).

Print Articles, Reports and Newspaper extracts

Alnwick Journal for 1860 and notes prepared by Vera Mallon for a Bailiffgate Museum Exhibition.
Alnwick Mercury newspaper for 24th October 1855
Amble and District History Website.
Baillie, David, Northumberland County Council, 'Restoration of former coal waste heaps' 1973 – 2007
C.W.S's in house magazine *Ourselves* for 1935 p 204.
Heavyside, Tom, *Railway Bylines*, May 1999 p 270.
Newcastle Journal, 'The Sinking of Shilbottle Pit' – article of Monday 15th March 1982.
Newcastle Guardian and Tyne Mercury, 19th July, 1862 p. 5 column 5.
Northumberland Gazette 5th March 1965, Northumberland Archives NRO 06994-18-25
Pevsner, Nikolas, *The Buildings of England, Northumberland*. Second Edition pp 568 -569.
Platten, Rt Rev Stephen A research article 'Borderlands', *The Berwick Advertiser and Berwickshire News* 27th June 2019 p. 19.
Wayman, Mr W.T., Plans and papers entitled *Specifications of Underground Coal Workings at Shilbottle Colliery* and *NCB Method Study papers report B243/W/8* referring to Whittle/Shilbottle Combination – 1976/77.

Internet articles
http://www.fusilier.co.uk/shilbottle_northumberland/history.htm

Introduction

I lived in Shilbottle for only six years until as a 16 year old I left to begin work as a police cadet in Northumberland in 1961. My father's family were natives of the village. He, like his father and grandfather, was a miner at the colliery. My wife was born in the village and my formative years were spent there playing football, cricket, roaming the back lanes and making long lasting friends.

During my research for this book I have been reminded that Shilbottle was described by locals as 'a village of "three halves", top, middle and bottom'. Those at the top rarely frequented the bottom and the nearest the bottom folk got to the top was St. James' Church, the fish shop not far from it and, before the Working Men's Club was built, the Farriers Arms.

In researching *Shilbottle – its past and its people* I have been on a journey of discovery unearthing facts about people, places, institutions and events which have stirred memories and established new affections. I have interviewed countless villagers, raided their collections of photographs and with gratitude, noted their stories.

My book follows a similar pattern to that of my previous book about the former colliery village at Bilton Banks. It covers the Parish of Shilbottle's early history, religion in the village, the schools, the Grange Pit and its later link with Whittle Colliery, military involvement, sports and social activities and commercial outlets. The final pages pay tribute to a few people in the village who have been honoured for their service and the contribution they have made to the village's life and history. Inevitably, in a book of this nature, I will have missed important facts or failed to uncover crucial information about people and events and for this I apologise.

In researching another book *CRAMLINGTON its past and its people*. I came across a piece written by a local historian in Cramlington. Towards the end of the last century, Alan Lowther wrote some words which are very relevant to this book:

> For any community, the store of traditional knowledge should be regarded as a valuable asset, a mirror, reflecting the on-going process of development and change in the social pattern of local life. Such knowledge provides an insight into understanding ... containing much that explains communal modes of thought, outlook and action; to a considerable extent nurturing each successive generation. An awareness of this helps contribute to the creation of identity and gives community a firmer base and consequently a clearer sense of purpose, ready to face up to and adapt to challenges of contemporary life.

I hope that this book achieves that purpose. It draws on archive material, personal accounts, reflections and anecdotes and I could not have written it but for the willingness of the remarkable people to share their verbal and written stories and to allow me to use their photographs.

I was down Shilbottle Grange Pit only once, with a school group when I was 14 years old. Even after that experience I failed to take proper interest in the nature and danger of my father's work. I am sure he would have been delighted to see this work in print and so it is to John Stewart's memory and to all the colliers of the Grange Pit that I dedicate this book.

Barry Stewart

Children sledging in Percy Road in the 1940s. *Julia Tweedy collection*

The History of Shilbottle Parish

Geographically Shilbottle parish lies south of Alnwick and is separated from that historic market town by the Cawledge Burn. Lesbury parish is situated to the north-east of the village and Warkworth parish is to the south-east. Brainshaugh and Felton are to the south. The land on which Shilbottle stands slopes upwards from the twin branches of the Cawledge Burn which are 212 feet above sea level and it rises to a ridge at the Beacon Hill which is 589 feet above sea level. The hill divides the valley of the River Aln from the valley of the River Coquet.

The parish of Shilbottle has an area of 6,501 acres and comprises the five Poor Law townships of Shilbottle, Shilbottle Woodhouse, Hazon and Hartlaw, Guyzance which is extra parochial, Whittle and Newton-on-the-Moor. The village of Shilbottle is between 410 and 489 feet above sea level and has a commanding view over the sea and the conurbations to the south.

Few traces of prehistoric habitation in and around Shilbottle have been found but a circular or oval camp made of stone and soil, with a diameter of 70 paces, surrounded by an *agger** was discovered to the south-west of the village in 1759.

Near Denemoor a greenstone axe hammer-head was found. In 1833 a Bronze Age food vessel dated between 3000 – 2000BC was found at Hazon. Bronze axe heads and jewellery have also been found in the Long Dene which runs between Longdyke and Woodhouse Farm.

On Beacon Hill, the site of the camp and *agger*, a bonfire was kept ready for signalling in Napoleonic times, and as part of the celebrations in connection with the Coronation of George V on 22nd June, 1911, a bonfire was lit.

The parish name of Shilbottle suggests a Saxon origin; *botel* meaning home; Shilbottle (Shilbottell) being named after the male Saxon leader Shil, alternatively known as Schiplinge.

'Shilbottell' is referred to in more detail in a survey carried out for the Earl of Northumberland during Queen Elizabeth 1st's reign, the township being described as being in the possession of 'William Barone Hilton'. Gilbert (Gisbright) Tison, occupied the position of standard bearer in the host of Normans which followed William the Conqueror in 1066. He shared in the lands taken from the Saxon owners. Hilton is said to have obtained the lordship of Shilbottle, Newton, Hazon and other habitations in the parish of Embleton. Gilbert Tison's son William succeeded him, and he, in his turn, was succeeded by his son German. German's daughter Beneta (or Bona) 'gained' Shilbottle by marriage to William Hilton, a baron of the Bishopric of Durham.

Shilbottell remained in the ownership of the Hilton family up to 21st March in either 1351 or 1352, but soon after this Shilbottell was acquired by Henry Percy, the first Earl of Northumberland. On 27th June 1405 King Henry IV granted Shilbottell to his son John along with other nearby estates, including Alnwick Castle. However, by 1472 Shilbottell was reacquired by the Earl of Northumberland.

Land in and around 'Shilbottel' (as the village was alternatively titled) was in the 15th century rented out by Earl Percy to 'free tenants'. A survey made in 1498 listed the tenants and land-holders, providing the size of their holding as:

Robert Hewgh	8 acres.
Gilbert Browne	3 acres.
The Church Wardens	2 acres.
The Abbot of Alnwick	2 husbandlands **
The Prior of the Order of St. John	4 acres.

There were also sixteen 'customary tenants' who held 'husbandland' of equal value. Six had holdings varying in size from 11 acres to 22 acres. Rents for these holdings varied between 6s 11d and 14s 8d per year. There were also four cottage tenants who paid a rent of 4s 2d per annum.

At the beginning of the 16th century another survey of the Percy estates showed freehold lands to be in the possession of Ellen Gallant (104 acres), John Harte (14 acres) Thomas Huntley (seven acres of land formerly belonging to the order of St. John of Jerusalem), and William Humble (five acres – belonging to the church). There were also nineteen tenant farmers, one Arthur Strother*** possessing two farms, and four cottage farmers, with smaller acreages at their disposal.

Several key people are mentioned in 15th century succession records. These include:

Thomas Doddesworth – Bailiff and Forester.
John Stamp – Keeper of the Wood.
Thomas Stamp and Robert Stampe of 'North and South Woode'.
Arthur Strother of Shilbottle.

A further survey made around 1567 by Earl Percy describes the *towne of Shilbottell as a very poor towne ... although they have much arable land.*

The survey adds that *There is within these fields of Shilbottell one coole myne which ys much profitable for the*

This history of Shilbottle, has been mainly extracted from http://www.fusilier.co.uk/shilbottle_northumberland/history.hlm; which relies heavily on Hodgson, John Crawford, FSA, History of Northumberland Vol V (Newcastle upon Tyne, Andrew Reid & Co Ltd) 1899.

*   An agger is an ancient roman rampart, or any artificial elevation. It is a Latin word – for an embankment that gave Roman roads the proper draining base – a ridge that supports the road surface.

**   A 'husbandland' was a notional measure of land, signifying a share in the township's manorial land rather than a precise measure.

*** The Strother family were wealthy property owners in Alnwick and elsewhere.

tenants there and to th' inhabitants of the townes thereabouts.

In 1585 the mine was still rented by William Gray of 'Alnwicke'.

Seventeen years later the mine was held under lease to Griffin Butler and William Harte.

In 1628 'Shilbottle Park' was granted to Martin Stamp and he held this by further lease for 21 years from 1649. When it expired there was a change of tenancy to Joseph Forster, who is thought to have been a member of the Low Buston family and an ancestor of the High Buston family of Newton by the Sea.

In 1663 the Wood-house, the colliery and part of Shilbottle's land belonged to the Earl of Northumberland. One of the earliest 17th century hand drawn maps of Shilbottle was used by the Earl of Northumberland's staff to determine the revenue they could demand from their employer's tenants to buy the Earl's freedom from imprisonment in The Tower of London.

In 1759 when Shilbottle Moor or Common was divided, an allotment of land was set apart for Woodhouse making it an independent township.

As part of the township of Shilbottle, Woodhouse, with an acreage of 571 in 1891, was not noticeably distinct from the rest of the township. It was, however, separately recorded, its population in 1891 being 31.

Left: An early 20th century image of Woodhouse farm cottages. The C.W.S. built colliery houses of Garden Terrace, west of Woodhouse, can just be seen beyond the two storey properties.

Early mining of Coal

During the 18th century the coal mines in the Parish of Shilbottle were held under successive leases by the Archbold family of Cawledge Park and Alnwick.

The Armstrong Map of 1760 clearly marks two blocks of 'Coal Houses' and ten dwellings near St. James' Church.

Collieries are also marked on a map of 1820 drawn by Frazer which shows a scattering of houses around Shilbottle's church and two collieries at Dean Moor and Whittle.

Greenwood's 1828 map of Northumberland shows Colliery Farm, and to the south, close to Hampeth, a 'Pit House' and below it 'Colliery House.'

Bulmer's 1887 *History and Directory of Northumberland* makes reference to the superior coal mined at Shilbottle and records that a lump was exhibited at the Edinburgh Exhibition of 1886.

A postcard produced for Shilbottle Coal Company's Longdyke Colliery advertises that:

Shilbottle Coals are acknowledged to be the Best House Coals produced. Durability, Heat and Freedom from Ash are their qualities.

Prominent people in Shilbottle village, referred to by Bulmer, at this time include:

Robert Brown	Publican, Percy Arms.
Ann Corbett	Dressmaker.
William Dysen	Schoolmaster.
Thomas Frater	Joiner.
Rev. Golightly	Vicar.
Jane Huntley	Grocer.
Robert Hudson	Gamekeeper for the Freelands of Shilbottle Old Pit.
Thomas Frater	Secretary Mechanics' Reading Room.
Richard Henderson	Librarian of the Mechanics' Reading Room.
Rob Angus Maule	Tailor.
Robert Muers	Publican and Blacksmith (The Farriers Arms).
James Plender	Grocer.
John Richardson	Cow Keeper.
Jowsy Richardson	Road Contractor.
John Riddell	Colliery Overman.
Thos John Riddell	Butcher.
John Roscamp	Colliery Manager (Shilbottle Collieries).
J Wilson	Manager Shilbottle Quarry.
Isabella Ternent	Dressmaker.
Robert Thompson	Foreman – Brick and Tile Works.
Robert Thompson	Carter.
Luke Weatheritt	Carter.
Elizabeth Weightman	Shopkeeper.
Jas John Wilson	Coal Agent.
Joseph Charlton	Farmer at Hitchcroft.
John Coxon	Farmer at Low Dyke.
John & Robert Frater	Farmers at Colliery Farm.
David Gladhome	Farmer at Town Farm.
Thomas Hutchinson	Farmer at Hill Head.
William Lough	Farmer at South East Farm.
William Robinson	Farmer.

The 1897 edition of *Kelly's Directory of Trades and Businesses* records that Earl Percy was still Lord of the Manor.

The chief landowner was Thomas Clutterbuck. Eighteenth and 19th century Poll Registers trace the Clutterbuck family through John of Craster in 1710 to John (junior) of Warkworth in 1826, the forebear of the chief landowner, Thomas Clutterbuck, referred to in Kelly.

The soil in and around Shilbottle at this time was described as *clayey, with lime and freestone subsoil.* The chief crops grown were barley, beans and peas. The township was recorded as being of 2,999 acres with a rateable value of £2,700. The population in 1891 was 454 while the population of the ecclesiastical parish was 766.

The *excellent coal mine and freestone quarry and tile manufactory* are referred to, as is the investment by Hugh Taylor* of £100, the *proceeds of which were to be distributed at Christmas among the poor of the village, without regard to religious persuasion.*

The 1860 (25 inches to 1 mile) Ordnance Survey map of Shilbottle village centre shows three public houses or inns; The Percy Arms at the head of North Side, The Farriers Arms at its present location at the top of South Side and the Black Swan Inn, almost opposite St. James Church and the Peel Tower. Below the Percy Arms is a Wesleyan Methodist chapel near the Church of England school.

The Farriers Arms which by 1897 was the only public house remaining in the village.

The following further notable people of Shilbottle are listed in *Kelly's Directory*, alongside their occupations:

James Buglass	Carrier.
William Leith	Tile manufacture.
Thomas Milburn	Stone Mason.
John Riddell	Farmer.
Miss Margaret Robinson	Shopkeeper.
William Robinson	Cattle Dealer.
Thomas Scott	Farmer at Longdyke.
Garwood, Paynter & Dunn	Shilbottle Coal Co.
Joseph Smailes	Carrier.
Thomas Telford	Carrier.
George Wm Truman	Joiner.
Mark Truman	Blacksmith.
James Wilson	Rate Collector.
Mark Gerrard	School master.

The Public School in Shilbottle was reported to have been endowed by the Duke of Northumberland and the trustees of the estate of Hugh Taylor, former coal mine owner. The school had capacity for 200 children, the average attendance being 177.

A photograph taken by Reverend Percy Lee on Coronation Day 22nd June, 1911, of the oldest and youngest inhabitants of Shilbottle:
Margaret Corbett born 1st October 1829;
George Young born 3rd September 1830;
Mary Storey born 1st October 1830,
and youngest
John Robert Mitchison born 28th May, 1911;
Kathleen Mackay born 17th March 1911
and George Edward Hardy born 19th May 1911.

---

*   Hugh Taylor was the third son of Thomas Taylor of Newburn, who was the Duke of Northumberland's mineral agent. Hugh, the second Duke of Northumberland, appointed Hugh Taylor as his colliery agent. The Taylor sons were all respected and well qualified colliery 'viewers' (engineers) or mine owners.

Hazon

The name Hazon seems to have been settled through centuries of changes. Hazon was initially held under the de Viscis and then the Percy family. The hamlet is first mentioned in an agreement, between Hugh of Heisende and German Tison in 1202, concerning 100 acres of woodland. Over time the name, having nothing to do with hazel trees, changed from Heisende, Haysand, Haysande to Hassand. By 1682 it had become Hazon, meaning a hedge end, boundary, or a sandy place by a hedge.

Robert and Elizabeth Lisle's stone which sits above the front door of Hazon House.
courtesy Christopher Lendrum, Hazon House

Hazon is described by Hodgson as a district of irregular form 2 miles by 2.25 miles, sloping south from the valley of the Coquet to an elevation of 425 feet above the sea. Its acreage was calculated to be 1,445.

Various court proceedings mention other occupants of Heisende (Hazon); the first in 1312 refers to Hugh de Heysand, who with others was accused of sheep stealing. Two centuries later, in 1524 the Manor Court of Shilbottel found a John Cowy of Haysand and a man named Alan, a servant of the priest of Shilbottel, guilty of affray 'when blood was shed.'

Some of the owners and occupiers of Hazon are known to have been:

- In 1559/60 Thomas Lisle of Elyhaugh who took Hassand on a lease.
- In 1582 Marmaduke Thirkeld who acquired the manor of Hassand.
- In 1669 Sir Henry St. Quintin of Yorkshire who inherited Hassand from his mother, the daughter of Marmaduke Thirkeld, who then sold it to Robert Lisle.
- In the 17th century Humphrey Lisle of Felton had possession of the house, which he passed to his son Robert.
- By 1684 Robert Lisle had virtually rebuilt the house for his marriage to Elizabeth. A stone marriage plate with the initials L (Lisle) R (Robert) and E (Elizabeth), with 1684 above the intitials, was positioned over the front door of the property.
- In 1715 Hazon was sold to William Lawson of Longhirst, who wanted to mine the coal beneath the manor. In 1861 the sole landowner was still William Edward Lawson, J.P.
- In 1880 – the manor house at Hazon was extensively improved with rooms being added to the back for the servants and a new wing built on the front.
- In the 20th Century, Hazon was sold to the Cooperative Society. The purchase was to allow the mining of coal across the area of Hazon.
- The mine manager lived in the house.

Census data for 1891 show the population to be 132; in 1851 it was 118. By 1881 it had increased 181. The soil was described in Kelly's survey as being similar to Shilbottle's, the main crops then being wheat, barley and turnips.

By 1861, following the development of the railways, mail was being received via Acklington where there was also a telegraph office.

Bulmer (1883) records the following notable people were active at Hazon.

Matthew Dixon Miller.
Margaret Green Dressmaker.
William Hopper Farmer at Hazon House.
James Huntley Farmer Hazon Lee
Robert, John & Thomas Shotton Farmers at Hazon High Houses.

In 1871 there were five family members and two servants resident in Hazon House. Matthew Dixon owned the mills at Hazon and Morwick, near Warkworth.

By 1891 there were six servants and a butler and his wife who lived at Hazon Mill, south of Hazon House. The farm steward and his family lived at Hazon Lea, also south of Hazon House. The census for 1871 describe the steward's wife and two teenage daughters 'as outdoor workers'.

To the north of the house, and west of Hazon Burn, there is evidence of medieval ridge and furrow land cultivation following an 'S' pattern. Above Hazon House, to the north-west, is the old mill race and granary. Further north at West Hazon is the former steward's house. The linked property next door is Hazon East, which had previously been three farm workers' cottages. All of the properties are Victorian in design, as are two smaller cottages on the opposite side of the road leading to Hazon House.

At Hazon House there are the remains of a walled kitchen garden and a densely wooded area enclosing stables, a former piggery and coach house built by the Lawsons.

In 1930 – Hazon was sold to the Bell brothers, who farmed High and Low Hazon. The owners in 2020 were Christopher and Margaret Lendrum.

Hartlaw

Hartlaw, commonly linked with Hazon because of its proximity, is a farm of 287 acres on a 400 foot contour line, with a view over the Coquet to Longhorsely Moor to the west, Cresswell Point to the south-east and Coquet Island to Low Buston to the east. It is described in Bulmer's directory as having *a goodly 17c house on an eminence, two stories in height*.

Hartlaw separates the estate given in 1684 by Robert Widdrington to his nephew of the same name. In 1883, George Alder was the farmer there.

Guyzance

The township of Guzance, on the River Coquet has an area of 1,332 acres. It is located between Shilbottle and Acklington. On the green vale or haugh, three miles from the mouth of the Coquet, there was the historic church of 'St. Wilfred of Gysnes.' There is still evidence of a convent sited next to the ruined abbey at that location; the latter having Norman or Transitional architecture.

After the Reformation and the confiscation of church lands and possessions, the monastic property passed into secular hands. The inhabitants continued to bury their dead among the ruins of the priory. The district became extra parochial and was treated as such by the Tithe Commissioners in 1837, the land becoming the property of Mr T. Tate who with the Duke of Northumberland held ownership of land across Guyzance.

The inhabitants of Guyzance in 1837 were:

Ann Beal	Shopkeeper.
James Davidson Esq.,	of Bank House.
Margaret Gordon	Day School.
Harry Dobson,	Quarryman.
Samuel Heatley	Land Agent's Clerk.
William Johnson,	Joiner/Cartwright.
Thomas McKenzie	Joiner/Cartwright.
John Tate Esq.	Land Agent, Barn Hill.
Geo and John Tate	Joiners.
Thomas Thompson,	Blacksmith.
Ralph Trobe	Cow keeper, Guyson Cottage.
John Wilson	Miller, Guyzance Mill.
Francis Dalrymple Wood	Gardener, Bank House.

The Farmers of Guyzance were:

Fargus Clark	Guyzance East House.
George Coxon,	Guyzance Lee.
George Martin,	Brainshaugh.

The Township of Newton on the Moor

Newton on the Moor was established as a borough (i.e. allowed to hold a market) in 1249. The ancient township was originally held by the Hilton family but by 1250 it had come into the possession of Rametta, daughter of John le Viscount. The village was then called Newton Supra Moram. Rametta gave her Northumberland estate to Simon de Montfort, Earl of Leicester, in exchange for lands in the South.

In 1269 Henry III gave the Barony of Embleton to his younger son Edmund, Earl of Lanchester. The Barony included Newton on the Moor which had been confiscated to the Crown on Simon de Montfort's death. In the 14th century the whole of the Parish of Shilbottel passed into the hands of the Percy family.

Over succeeding years, the village was owned by various families, among them John de Stanyington, Roger de Wyderyington and by the 1600s, George Lisle. In 1617 when George Lisle died, his lands at Newton went to his nephew, Lancelot Strother. In 1670 the 'Lordship Town' of Newton on the Moor was sold for £600 by Thomas Forster of Adderson to Edward Cook of Amble, who in his will, dated 31st December 1691, gave the south side of Newton on the Moor to his son Samuel. Samuel died in 1692 and Newton on the Moor fell into the possession of Edward Cook's son, Joseph. In 1772 Joseph's son, Samuel Cook, built Newton Hall on the site of an earlier house. Samuel Cook's grandson, Captain Samuel Edward Cook, R.N., inherited the Hall and estate from his maternal grandmother, who was the daughter and heiress of Robert Widdrington and sister and heiress of Reverend Doctor John Barker, D.D., Master of Christ's College, Cambridge. Samuel Edward Cook immediately assumed the name Widdrington.

On Samuel Edward Cook/Widdrington's death, in 1850, Newton Hall and other real estate went to Captain Widdrington's nephew Shallcross Fitzherbert Jacson. In 1880 he bought the remaining land at Newton on the Moor from Mr William G. Strother. Through wills and deeds transferring property in and around Alnwick and Warkworth, the Strother family can be traced to the 18th century.

One such document, dated 21st November 1769, is an agreement by

> Thomas Embleton, to pay the sum of 1 penny per year to Jane Strother, as penalty for resting his new-build property on her garden wall.

Major Shallcross Fitzherbert Widdrington.
courtesy Northumberland collections

The Widdrington family can be traced to a time before the Norman Conquest and it is known that the first Lord Widdrington fought on the side of Charles 1st at the Battle of Wigan in 1651 when he was overpowered by Parliamentary forces. Major Shallcross Fitzherbert Widdrington (*left*) mentioned in Kelly, originally had the surname Jacson but took the name Widdrington when his wife's maternal uncle Captain Samuel Widdrington died.

Shallcroft Fitzherbert Widdrington followed the Widdrington tradition of holding high office in Northumberland. A moderate

Conservative and ardent imperialist, he became a Justice of the Peace and was appointed High Sheriff of Northumberland in 1874.

Newton on the Moor is the highest and most westerly portion of the Parish of Shilbottle and is built on the north-east-facing side of Swarland Hill as it slopes down to Hazon Burn, a tributary of the River Coquet. Its position offers it protection from prevailing westerly winds and it is relatively sheltered. Kelly's 1861 directory describes Newton on the Moor as having *beautiful views of the German Ocean*. There was a quarry, initially marking the east end of the village. The only public buildings beyond the settlement were two public houses, the now Cook and Barker, and The Quarry, each with a smithy attached. It is from the quartered arms of the Cook and Barker families that the present Inn in Newton on the Moor takes its name. Several of the cottages date from the 18th century. The village had two larger houses; the Old Manor House and the Reading Room, both initially two storeys high.

Tenant farmers in and around Newton on the Moor in 1861 included John Lisle, Robert Smith, Thomas Scott, Isabel Jamyson, Edward Johnson and Thomas Cook of Brainshaugh.

The 1860 Ordnance Survey map shows industrial areas with lime kilns and quarries to the west of the village and below it to the east. Coal shafts are evident in the region of Fairlawns, situated south-west of the Cook and Barker and at Newton Colliery, which is referred to in greater detail later.

Clay was also extracted locally and there was a tile works at Newton Lowsteads. Tiles for the red pantiled roofs, which are a part of the special character of the village, are thought to have been produced locally.

Kelly comments that the township's Jubilee Hall was built in 1887 and was used chiefly as a mission hall for weekly services, regular concerts and public meetings. Also in the village was a reading room stocked with 500 volumes.

The reading room was reduced from a two storey building to one, as was the Old Manor House, in 1887, to give a 'model village' effect.

In 1842, towards the west end of the village a Methodist 'New Connexion' Chapel was built on a site given by Major Widdrington. The chapel has now been converted into a private dwelling.

The only commemorative monument in the village is a pant [well] at the east end, which was erected in 1914. It bears the inscription – 'ERECTED, by the TENANTS of NEWTON on the MOOR, to COMMEMORATE, the GOLDEN WEDDING of S.FITZHERBERT & CECILIA WIDDRINGTON, 20th APRIL 1804 -1964'.

The Bulmer and Kelly directories of 1887 and 1897 respectively, list the following prominent people resident in Newton on the Moor:

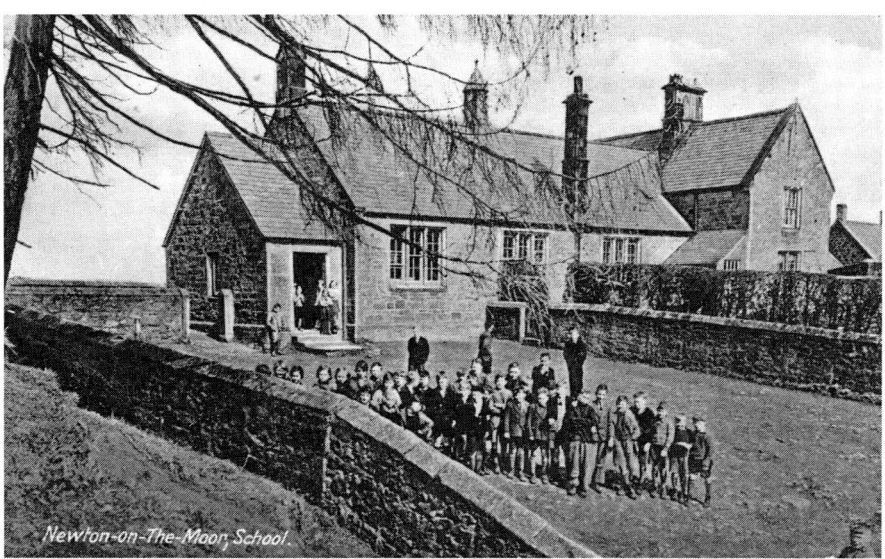

The Village School, at the west end of the village was built at the expense of landowners and supported by the Strother family with a £100 annual endowment. The school is also now a private dwelling.
Author's collection

Newton on the Moor Jubilee Hall.

Stephen Eastern	Sub Post Master.
Thomas Carr	Cow keeper.
Joseph Eastern	Grocer, Draper and Newsagent.
William Gowan	Lime Burner.
John McKenzie	Joiner/Cartwright.
James Oliver	Grocer.
Joseph Potts	Schoolmaster.
Andrew Scott	Viewer (Newton Colliery).
William Potts	Librarian at Newton Reading Room.
Thomas R Forster	Blacksmith and Publican at The Cook & Barker.
Robert Snaith	Blacksmith.
George Yarston	Tailor.
James Oliver	Carrier.
Robert Thos Coxon	Farmer at Home farm.
Joseph Givens	Farmer at Low Newton Hall.
Thomas Lough	Farmer at Newton Villas.
John Richardson	Farmer at Newton North Farm.
Robert Trobe	Farmer at Sunnyside.

Lord Nelson's obelisk

Straddling the boundary of Swarland and the south edge of Newton on the Moor stands a freestone obelisk erected in 1807 by Alexander Davison, in memory of his friend Horatio Nelson, later First Viscount Nelson, victor of the Battle of Trafalgar.

Alexander Davison made his fortune in Canada, where he met the 24 year old Nelson who was commanding HMS *Albermarle* which was docked in Quebec during the American War of Independence. He represented Nelson in a naval tribunal dealing with the distribution of the spoils of war. The obelisk bears three inscriptions. The first is Nelson's direction to his seamen: *England expects every man to do his duty*. The second commemorates Nelson's success in the Battle of Trafalgar on 21st October 1895; and the third is a personal tribute by Davison. This says,

> Not to commemorate the public virtues and heroic achievements of Nelson, which is the duty of England; but to the memory of private friendship; this erection is dedicated by Alexander Davison of Swarland Hall.

A line of trees in Swarland estate is laid out as a further tribute to Nelson's achievements in the Nile Delta. The trees were positioned to indicate the location of the French and British ships which were then engaged in the Battle of the Nile.

In 1891 the population of Newton on the Moor was 215, the township then comprising a smattering of small cottages around the square and the Cook and Barker public house, and more grandly Newton Hall, Newton Villa and North Newton.

The Cook and Barker Inn *c.*1900.

The Cook and Barker Inn 2020

The Township of Whittle

The name Whittle seems to have derived from Walter de Wytehill* who held the place in the 13th and 14th centuries. In 1715 the township comprised 549 acres. It was described as *a mean village on ascent.*** On 29th March 1715 the burgesses of Whittle sold the township to John Clutterbuck as part payment for an estate at Walker on Tyne.

At the beginning of the 19th century the population was 101. In 1891 it was down to only nine.

The whole township was within the farmland of William Lough and later his sons.

Farms in the 19th Century

Early parish records show that the predominant occupation of men was that of agricultural labourer or servant, but by 1801 parish baptism registers contain the occasional entry showing the child's father to be 'pitman'. By 1814 most pages in baptism registers for Shilbottle show that half of the fathers' occupations were 'pitman' or miner.

In the 19th century, across the parish of Shilbottle there were 22 farms, some of which crossed the parish boundaries of Alnwick, and Lesbury and Warkworth.

High Buston	Low Buston (with Buston Barns).
Brotherwick	Southside.
Woodhouse	Townfoot.
South East Farm	Hartlaw.
Sturton Grange	Shortridge.
Colliery Farm	Village Farm.
Longdyke	Cawledge Park.
West Cawledge Park	Hazon High Houses.
Low Whittle	High Whittle.
Hall's Farm	Green's Farm.
Shiel Dyke	Tweedy's Stead.

---

* Also referred to as Gilbert de Vhill and Walter de Quyhill and subsequently in 1296 Walter de Whithille. A further name change is shown as Whitley.

** Hodgson, John Crawford, FSA, *History of Northumberland Vol V* p 473 (Newcastle upon Tyne, Andrew Reid & Co Ltd) 1899.

The First Edition OS map shows how much the acreage of the farms varied. Southside had 114.153 acres, Newton on the Moor 939.834 acres; collectively Low Buston and Buston Barns 898.609, whereas Brotherwick had only 185.889 acres.

The Duke of Northumberland is the landlord for the majority of farms across the parish of Shilbottle. Farmhouses, outbuildings and tenancy agreements therefore followed a similar pattern. The tenant farmers did have some freedom however, to work their land in a method most likely to accrue profit for themselves their family and the Duke. The Stokoe family at Town Foot Farm, for instance, whilst maintaining livestock on their land, diversified in the late 1950s and began rearing chickens on a large scale.

The soil quality across the parish differs considerably, from heavy clay to very sandy, and this has influenced how the farm prospered and modified its methodology.

In the early part of the 20th century many itinerant workers came to the rural community at the busiest times of the farming calendar and they would be found working in the fields bringing in crops. During the Second World War, with many of the farm workers called up to fight, it fell to young women to work on the farms and many village girls joined the Women's Land Army.

Farming is a full time occupation requiring dedicated and skilled craftsmen and women to get the best from the land, and local farms have produced some remarkably successful people, some of whom diversified in unexpected directions. Henry Brewis* for instance, who could trace his farming ancestry back to 1590, in addition to being a successful farmer, wrote many humorous stories which despite his death in 2000 still find their way into *The Northumbrian Magazine*. His unique selling point was his ability to write coherent English, peppered with broad, humorous but understandable dialect, which was pithy, pertinent, often poetic with a political point to make. His prose was broken up with his artwork, cartoons and illustrations and in his writing he was successful and prolific.

His *Arrivedercci Shilbottle* provides a classic example:

> Talk to any farmer these days and he'll tell you he's pretty fed up.
>
> "Oh really." I hear you snigger. "So what's fresh? Farmers always grumble don't they?" If it's not the weather, it's the government, the collie dog, the lambing or the long-suffering wife. Maybe the whole lot at once. There's either a drought or there's too much rain. The missus wants ANOTHER frock (her second since the coronation)! Moss is in pup to that Doberman cross-Dachshund from the vicarage. The sheep are wandering about in the barley field and the government is wandering about in disarray. Farmers have a well earned reputation as premier league complainers. It is the very nature of the job – not least because Mother Nature can always foil the best laid plans of the most imperturbable peasant.
>
> But now there's something else to grouse about, something even more soul destroying and sinister than set-aside, salmonella, or beef on the bone.
>
> Recently a new all-consuming pest has descended on the countryside. A locust-like plague of paper is blowing over from the continent and threatens to suffocate life as we once knew it. There are now so many forms, maps and questionnaires to fill in that some farmers are spending all their working day stuck in an office. Those ruddy weather beaten complexions grow pale, wellies stand forlorn and abandoned at the door, hard gnarled hands, once the size of shovels, shrivel to slender effeminate things with clean fingernails.... as he is on the phone, nervously chewing a biro, sobbing pitifully into his pocket calculator, as he tries to comprehend the mountain of ambivalent gobbledegook churned out by the MAFFia.**

Henry Brewis was related to Richard and Michael Brewis, tenant farmers of Woodhouse Farm and the account which follows provides a clear account of life on Woodhouse Farm and the history of farming there.

Woodhouse Farm

The following detailed account of Woodhouse Farm, its tenants and its development, has been drawn from presentation notes provided by Richard Brewis following his talk to Shilbottle Local History Group in 2019. It traces the farm's history from the 16th century and illustrates how farming methods changed over those years which whilst particular to one farm in the parish, will reflect the changes other farmers were obliged to make over more than 400 years.

'Woodhouse Farm was originally called Shilbottle Park. In 1585 there were two large, well stocked woods on the farm land, much of the timber had been thinned out for use by the Duke of Northumberland, or

Woodhouse Farm – taken from the air in 1969.
Courtesey Richard Brewis, Woodhouse Farm

---

* Henry Brewis 1932 -2000. His books, Published by Powdene Publishing and Farming Press, include *A stroll in the Country*, *Chewing the Cud*, *Country Dance*, *Don't Laugh till he's out of sight*, *Night Shift*, and *A Little nonsense about sheep*.
** Excerpt from *A Stroll in the Country*, (Newcastle, Powdene Publishing, 1999), p64.

The distinctive chimney in closer detail, which was for the coke and coal fired boiler which powered a steam engine used for driving threshing and turnip pulverising machines.

exchanged by the 'keeper of the wood', Thomas Stamp, for corn. By 1607 the lease for Shilbottle Park passed to Robert Stamp and this included a dwelling house on the current farm site. The farm then had 60 acres of arable land, 40 acres of grass meadow, 84 acres of rough pasture and 164 acres of woodland, the latter of which, over 22 years, had reduced from 330 acres. By 1612 Stamp was superseded by Arthur Strother of Shilbottle, but by 1628 the farm had been restored to the Stamp family, Martyn Stamp, the son, gaining the lease. Twenty one years later the farm passed to Joseph Foster who held a number of farms including the adjoining farm of Low Buston. His descendants held the tenancy until 1775.

During the Foster period at Woodhouse the present farm house was built and an annex added around 1720.

The small building at the top of the aerial picture of Woodhouse was a smithy, fully equipped for the travelling farrier/blacksmith. The buildings immediately below the smithy were the stables for the farm horses.

The tenants of Woodhouse, as it became, included

1775	Thomas Graham and W. Allen.
1781	Henry Potts.
1812	John and William Potts (who were also skilled land surveyors and map makers.
1847	William Fenwick who also held the tenancy of South Side near Sturton Grange.
1860	W Rand.
1884 -1888	there was not a tenant but the land may have been let to grazers.*
1889	Mr Thomas Samuel Brewis**, from New Moor at Ashington.

When young Thomas Samuel Brewis took up the tenancy on Lady's Day, 25th March 1889, the farm had been unoccupied for five years and it was dilapidated, run down and overgrown with gorse and thistles which had to be removed by hand. Unlike the surrounding farmsteads which had easy to work and cultivate sandy soil, Woodhouse stood in a basin. The few inches of top soil were workable, but beneath was thick clay which was almost impervious. Consequently, the farmland was often very wet and occasionally flooded.

T.S. Brewis came to the farm as a bachelor, aged 27. He married Isabella Clark in November 1889. By 1901 his tenancy agreement records that the farm land had 300 acres of permanent grass and 200 acres in arable rotation (oats for animal feed, barley for malt, and turnips). By 1914 wheat was being grown 'for the war effort'.

The tenancy agreement prohibited the sale of all but livestock and corn at the farm, so the money earners then were fatted beef cattle, lambs, malting barley and wool.

In the 1840s the farm buildings were expanded to accommodate immature store cattle brought into Alnwick or Acklington marts from Ireland or Scotland and walked back to the farm to fatten on grass in the summer, and hay, 'swede' turnips and oats over winter.

In the 1840s Irish labourers were brought to the farm to extensively drain the pasture using hand-shaped clay pipes.*** These proved very effective and extended the amount of pasture and arable land available for cultivation and grazing.

The drier land also meant that it was less often necessary to bring the cattle into the cow-sheds during winter.

T.S. Brewis

In the 1920s electricity was introduced to the farm, which was easy to arrange as the Grange Colliery was close by. The C.W.S. who owned the pit, took 25 acres of land from Woodhouse for the mine site, the railway and waste heap.

A dairy enterprise was introduced for up to twelve milking cows. The milk was sold wholesale or to residents of the growing village.

Thomas and Isabella Brewis had eight children and all six of their sons became tenant farmers and their two daughters married wealthy farmers on local farms.

---

*   *Memories of Shilbottle*, Millenium Edition, p13 indicates that the residence at Woodhouse in 1887 was in the possession of Farmer James Huggup.
**   The Brewis family tree shows name Brewis was derived from Thomas Brewhouse, 1630 – 1703. Between 1699 and 1729, under Samuel Brewes the surname had been reduced, and by 1729 a vowel change made it Brewis, the now accepted name.
***   Richard Brewis, when interviewed in January 2020, praised the efficiency and durability of the ancient pipes. They seldom failed but when they blocked, the surrounding flooding became obvious and relatively simple to correct. The workmen 'camped' in the barns between shifts.

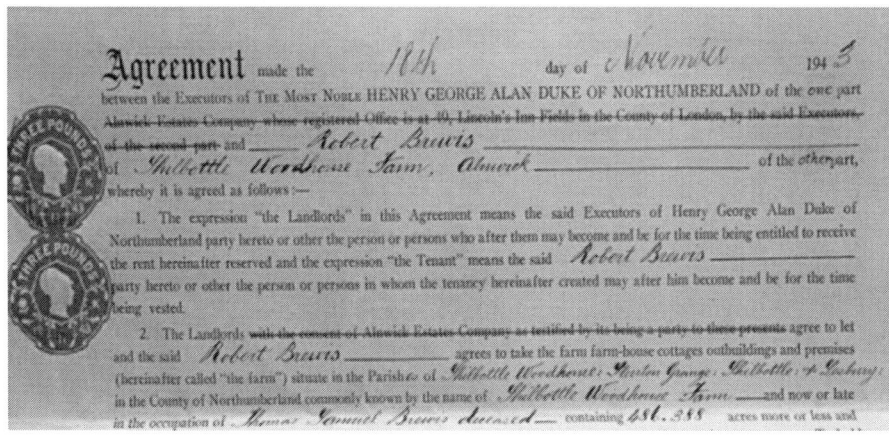
Robert Brewis's tenancy agreement for Woodhouse Farm.

In 1933 T.S. Brewis went into partnership at Woodhouse with his youngest son Robert ; although the partnership continued to be dominated by T.S. Brewis. Robert, in addition to being a most competent farmer, was an accomplished pianist and accordion player, and as part of a dance band, toured local village halls. It was not until the death of T.S. Brewis's wife in 1941 that Robert was permitted to move with his wife and family out of one of the nearby farm cottages, to care for his failing father, who died in the Spring of 1943.

During the Second World War, wheat was grown at Woodhouse as part of the war effort, and to compensate for the loss of farm workers who were conscripted, four Italian prisoners of war, were housed at the farm and employed as labourers. After their period of labour four German prisoners of war, who were excellent workers, were bused in daily.*

In 1943, following the death of his father T.S. Brewis, Robert Brewis took over the tenancy of Woodhouse in his own right.

In 1944 a British Army training unit was based at the farm, living in the outbuildings.

They dug trenches opposite the farm house and drove tanks up and down the road. The officers were accommodated in the farm house.

In 1946 tractors started to take over from horses and the horse stables were converted into a large milking byre as the farm was by then basically a dairy farm with small beef and arable enterprises.

Robert Brewis and Margaret Ann (Peggy), his wife had three children and on 25th March 1963 their son Michael was authorised by the Duke of Northumberland to be joint tenant of Woodhouse. This was after he had completed an agricultural degree course at Kings College, Newcastle. Michael, the first Brewis to be academically qualified as a farmer, was ably supported by his wife Janet (née Mitchell). The farm quickly changed. It ended milk and beef production, leaving it as an efficient sheep and arable unit. Several old pasture fields were converted to arable and two fences were removed to create larger fields into arable for crop production.

The cropping area rose during the 70s and 80s to 380 acres. EU membership and subsidies, together with new cropping possibilities for winter barley, winter oilseed rape, spring beans and stubble turnips to be used as sheep feed (sold to a shepherd renting 200 acres) massively increased productivity and profit. Enhanced fertilisers and crop protection made higher yields possible. A local contractor cultivated and sowed the farm's crops. Farm staff fertilised, sprayed, harvested and stored the harvested crops.

A new shed was erected in 1986 which was used for housing sheep in the winter and for storing grain following harvest.

In 1973 Michael's sister Isobel was unlawfully killed on the farm and this devastated Michael and his family.

In 1986 Michael and Janet's son Richard gradually assumed responsibility for the running of the farm. This was after his return from Edinburgh University, where he too had completed a degree in agriculture.

South East Farm

South East Farm house was built in 1857 and is typical of the dwellings occupied by the Duke of

South East Farm, the outbuildings in the foreground beyond the farm house were also typical, but the larger white roofed hayshed was added in the 1970s.

---

* The Italian Prisoners were from a camp at Low Buston. In 1944 they were replaced by German prisoners from a camp at Longframlington.

Northumberland's tenant farmers. The Lough family have been tenants for over 100 years.

The hay storage areas were once subject to an arson attack, when a servant girl with mental health issues set fire to two stacks on 11th September, 1909 causing over £500 worth of loss. The following Week the *Northumberland Gazette* reported that:

> a young woman from Sleekburn, 20 years of age, employed as a servant girl with Mr Lough at South Farm has been charged not only with setting fire to haystacks but also maliciously setting fire to farm buildings the property of His Grace the Duke of Northumberland, being cattle sheds and a calf house, in part of which were six calves and the other part some hay. The plaintiff admitted setting fire to the stack with a lighted candle.

The next week the newspaper reported the case heard at Newcastle's Petty Sessions and stated that:

> the servant ... under observation in the hospital of Newcastle Prison was declared to be of unsound mind and an order was made by the Bench for her admission to the County Lunatic Asylum. No evidence in relation to the charges was presented against her.

Church Farm

It was close to Church Row and was so named because of its proximity to the Methodist Chapel at the west end of North Side.

Alice Robinson (née Smith), on the steps of Village Farm, with a young woman, believed to be Jane Patton in the foreground. *Keith Wilson collection*

Village farm

The farm was close to St. James' Church and in the 1960s was tenanted by the Provost family. The buildings have now been converted into a health and recreation centre. Diversification was not uncommon once mechanisation replaced manpower. The workers' cottages, no longer needed, were converted in the late 19th century into holiday homes, to provide additional income for the landlord.

These horses, pictured at Colliery Farm in 1913, were shortly afterwards commandeered for the war effort and shipped to France. *Gordon Straughan's collection*

Census data for Shilbottle between 1801 and 1991 shows how the township developed over 200 years:

Shilbottle Township
Year	Homes	Male	Female	Total
1801		229	243	472
1811		215	250	465
1821		259	289	548
1831	125	280	277	557
1841	115	262	287	549
1851	119	302	299	601
1861	115	283	287	570
1871	104	270	258	528
1881	82	-	-	428
1891	92	228	226	454

Shilbottle Civil Parish
Year	Homes	Male	Female	Total
1901	87	224	203	427
1911	89	228	195	423
1921	101	280	230	510
1931	244	585	503	1088
1941	-	-	-	-
1951	383	708	670	1378
1961	540	967	895	1862
1971	555	915	874	1789
1981	587	782	791	1573
1991	588	682	715	1397

Since the 1991 census Shilbottle has seen a great influx of newcomers and modern housing estates have been built opposite Percy Road east of the church and beneath the Farriers Arms.

Arthur, Rene and Andy Inglis, three future key people in the social life of the village, photographed outside Shilbottle's Council School in 1933. *Sandra and Blly McKnight collection*

Opening day of the new lounge of Shilbottle Working Men's Club.

Coal Mining in Shilbottle

Shilbottle's coalfield

Visitors to the parish of Shilbottle will find little evidence of coal mining and yet beneath the ground there remain tunnels many miles from the shafts where men, and earlier boys, entered the ground and travelled to 'win' coal, often several miles from the shaft bottom. But in addition to verbal accounts given by former miners and their photographs, the evidence is there in maps and records. Ordnance Survey surface maps, produced in 1966 and superimposed throughout by colliery surveyors and managers, show the workings of the various collieries across the parish. These reveal a total of 79 shafts, 74 of which are located between the Keeper's Pit north of Shilbottle village and up to 4 miles away to a midway point between the Newton Burn and Shiel Dyke in the west. Of the other five shafts, two were at Longdyke Pit at Bilton Banks, two at Shilbottle Grange pit and one south-east of Swarland. This was a pumping shaft.

The same maps show the extent of organised underground coal extraction from Longdyke Colliery between 1880 and 1925 under Bilton Banks, right up to Wooden Farm in the east until 1947, and in the north-west of Newton on the Moor from the Hunter and Riddel Pits. Prior to and including 1948, coal was being extracted west of High and Low Buston Farms in the east, the seams being accessed via Shilbottle Grange Pit. Mining in the west of the coalfield beneath the parish was similarly extensively mined between 1960 and 1978 towards Brainshaugh, and up to 1985 under the approaches to Acton House near Felton. The ground beneath Swarland Wood in the west and towards Hampeth Bridge, a little to the north, was also extensively mined from Whittle between 1970 and 1986. In the east until 1970 the mining from Shilbottle Grange went beneath High Hazon House under the River Coquet beyond Howlet and the Hermitage Farm.

The history of coal mining in Shilbottle Parish

Coal mining in and around Shilbottle has a long history. By the end of the 2nd century the Romans were extracting coal from most of the coalfields across England and Wales.* By the 13th century, coal was being shipped from Newcastle to London; and from the beginning of the Industrial Revolution in 1760, when hand tools were being replaced by machinery across the developing world, coal and steam took over

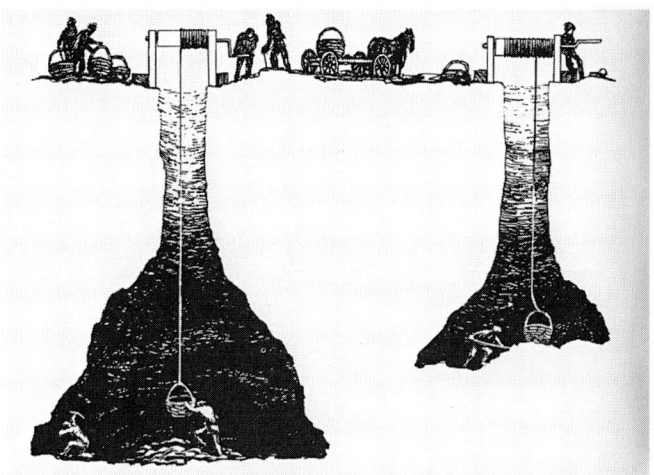

Sketch of a bell pit**.

from water and wind power. In the 18th century Britain was producing over 80% of the world's coal.

Bell pits were the earliest pits and were common across Northumberland.

These were dug down until the roof and walls were likely to collapse, whereupon a similar pit on an adjacent or near site was sunk.

Ventilation, in a 'blackdamp' atmosphere, almost without oxygen but with a mixture of carbon dioxide, nitrogen and water vapour, was a major safety issue for the underground workmen.*** Some modified bell pits, in the region of Ford, close to the Scottish border, were still in operation at the beginning of the 20th century.

Records show that by 1869 there were 139 collieries in the Northumberland Coalfield.

In Shilbottle there are three seams of coal: Townsend, Cannel and Shilbottle. The coal 'winning' area comprised an island bounded on the eastern side by the Great Whin Sill Dyke and to the south by the Hauxley Fault.

From the 16th century a number of small collieries in Shilbottle were producing coal.

In 1585 these included, unnamed mines owned by William Gray and William Bednell. The same mines in 1692 were owned by Griffin Butler and William Hart. In 1685 Whittle Colliery was owned by Thomas Gilbert, Gilbert Swinhoe and later Thomas Davison and Matthew Jefferson. At the beginning of the 18th Century around Deanmoor, Whittle and Shilbottle mines were leased by the Archbold family from Cawledge Park. Records**** (formerly in possession of

---

*   See 'Stewart, Barry; *Bilton Banks- The Pit and Its People*, Stenlake Publishing, Ayrshire, 2012 pp 4 – 44.
**   Northumberland County Council, Plessey, *The Story of a Northumberland Woodland* (N.C.C., Hexham, 1984) p.12.
*** See also Muckle, William, *No Regrets*, (Newcastle, People's Publications, 1981), p.19. 'Many's the time in my younger day, I would come home and could not eat anything. I would lie on the floor and sleep, dog tired from the bad air down the pit.'
**** An unsigned report entitled 'Coal Workings in Shilbottle Area', in the papers of Mr Terry Wayman, Under-manager at Shilbottle Colliery from 1965, referencing the North of England Institute and Messers W.S. Armstrong & Sons (mineral agents for the Duke of Northumberland) referring to tracings surveyed 25th April 1765 by Mr. Brown.

Mr Terry Wayman, Under-manager at the Grange Pit in Shilbottle) show that a pit had been sunk near to Dean Moor, approximately one mile west of Shilbottle Village. From the site of this pit a road had been driven in a southerly direction, with pits sunk on the line of the water level, with numerous small air shafts on the rise side of the road. A map produced for the 1st Duke of Northumberland, Hugh Percy* on 14th April 1764, shows a network of 54 coal borings to the west of Shilbottle Village. Sixteen of these produced coal, the others were either downcast to provide ventilation or were sunk in search of coal. The depth of the pit on the 18th century map was recorded as being dug to a depth of 13 fathoms, a fathom being 6 feet or 1.8 metres. As the colliers moved further south towards Felton the depth of the mines progressed to 70 fathoms.

The Duke of Northumberland's map shows an area representing a coalfield of 75 acres east of Hampeth and it is known that in 1764 there was a 'Windmill Pit' west of Deanmoor, 750 yards north of the Hampeth Bridge, and managed by Mr Archbold. This pit is believed to have opened on 22nd June 1763.

Prior to 1760 the collieries were worked by Alnwick Corporation. After 1762 these mines passed into the ownership of the Duke of Northumberland.

Deeper mines were sunk in and around Shilbottle. There were six shafts around Blue Lodge Farm, the first sunk around 1780. Three of the pits were named Hatchet, Hawley and Smokey and operated until the beginning of the 19th century. They worked the Townsend seam and used two shafts, the deepest of which went to a depth of 216 feet with a main seam of 32 inches.

In 1807 the Blue Lodge shaft at Colliery Farm, 2.5 miles south of Alnwick, was sunk. The alternative names for this pit, positioned 395 feet above sea level, were Engine, New East and Furnace. The pit shaft at Blue Lodge was 10 feet in diameter, twice that of previous pit shafts in the area. A coal seam 4 inches thick was encountered 142 feet below the surface and more significantly, in a seam of 3 feet 6 inches at 158.75 feet, with further narrow seams beneath. In the Shilbottle seam, at a depth of 274 feet, there was another workable layer of coal 2 feet 7 inches thick.

The workings of this pit (recorded in Mr Wayman's unattributed note) were headings 60 feet apart, 6 feet wide with 'bords'** 15 feet wide, leaving pillars 9 feet 9 inches wide to support the roof. A plan dated 16th November 1814 shows that workings from the pit at Blue Lodge went to a lower level and were worked right under the old village of Shilbottle. Originally coal in these early pits, was drawn from the coal face by sledges carrying low baskets which were brought to the 'coup' (the tipping point, pronounced cowp) where the coal was put into larger baskets on trains pulled by ponies to the shaft bottom. The baskets were drawn to the surface by hook on the end of a rope. In earlier times the rope would be lowered by means of a horse gin and later by steam engines.

Cages for tubs do not appear to have been used until the Longdyke Pit started.***

The Duke of Northumberland issued an amended lease in 1796 for a colliery to be worked at Bilton Banks. The demise of Longdyke Colliery, as it was known, in 1925 led to the sinking of Shilbottle Grange Pit. Both of these pits are referred to in greater detail in later paragraphs. Meanwhile, other pits were sunk and worked in and around Shilbottle.

Around 1830 a new shaft was sunk halfway between Shilbottle and Bilton Banks. This pit known as the Keeper's Pit**** was sunk near Town Foot Farm on the unclassified Alnwick to Shilbottle road. This allowed workings to be accessed towards the Blue Lodge seams in a southerly direction. There was a steam engine in this pit, driving a ventilator, to allow workings away from the shaft to be exploited.

An article about an arranged visit to the colliery, published in 1860 in The *Alnwick Journal* and summarised in 2019 by Miss Vera Mallon for the Bailiffgate Museum in Alnwick, captures the scene in descriptive and occasional romantic language, far removed from the everyday language of 'pitmen' whose daily experience was a more dangerous and dramatic adventure.

> Approaching nearer, the furnaces and machinery assumed the appearance of a steamer locked among fields of snow in the arctic regions. Passing several carts leading coals, we stood in a very dirty area of small coal, mud, water and rotten miscellaneous debris ploughed into muddy ridges; then by a circumbendibus around the engine house we arrived at a wooden staircase, something of the same species as mountebanks† at country fairs affix in front of their caravans.
>
> We mounted, and stood by the margin of the pit – an ugly looking hole – circular in shape, divided by boarding down the centre or diameter. On one side the pump was working; on the other side baskets full of coals were rising and being emptied by the banksman†† into carts, while empty ones were descending. We presented our credentials to the banksman, Buglass by name, who looked very good humoured through the black coal dust which obscured the 'human face divine', and, while he was getting ready to let us down, we divested ourselves of superfluous garments. We then slipped our leg through a loop in the chain, and with a companion to steady the descent, we were rapidly lowered into utter darkness. Of a

---

*   Formerly Sir Hugh Smithson, married to Elizabeth the last Earl's granddaughter, took the name Percy and became the frist Duke.
**   'Bord' is a straight road or passageway driven at right angles to the main cleavage of coal in a coal mine.
***   Extracted from Mr Wayman's report.
****   So named because a game keeper's cottage was located near the shaft.
†   Mountebanks – an itinerant who held forth to an audience from a platform.
††   Banksman – an overseer working above ground.

sudden we felt dry land (or rather wet coal) and having released our limb from its shackles we stood at the bottom of the pit.

Men working this pit were lowered on a chain to which leather straps were attached for them to place one foot whilst the other was used to stop them bouncing against the shaft walls while being lowered.

'We were now taken in charge by a very intelligent lad, by name John Weightman, a platelayer in the pit who first pointed out the stables where several horses were kept – poor animals, condemned never more to see the light of day. They looked very comfortable however, and eyed us, we thought, somewhat inquisitively, as if curious to know what we were after. We were now led along the 'rolley way'*, about six feet in height, with a line of iron rails. By this main road, access is readily obtained to the more distant parts of the mine. At one place we were shown the place where a boy, called Snaith, was accidentally killed by the fall of stone from overhead.

A walk of about half a mile or more, sometimes plunging into runnels of water, sometimes meeting horses drawing trams with baskets full of coal, and sometimes stopping to examine a 'trouble', an entrance to old workings, a current of water, or a characteristic rock, by the dim light of a candle, we came to an elevated place called a coup or cope. Here we saw a motley crowd of black-faced boys with white teeth and merry eyes, and were greeted with a cheer.

Our future progress was certainly not very promising. It lay along the seam of coal, and was only twenty-eight inches from floor to roof. It was therefore necessary in some parts to creep along on hands and knees over small coals, which soon became anything but a pleasant exercise, and made us envy the sinners who were compelled to perform a pilgrimage with peas in their shoes. Part of the way was easy, but not much pleasanter.

Extended at length on a very little truck, we were shoved along very rapidly by a putter – this is a boy whose duty it is to put or push the coals through the low passages to the coup, where they are emptied into corves [baskets] and conveyed by horses to the bottom of the shaft. After some time spent thus alternately crawling and being hurled along in deep darkness, sometimes fearing we should get our brains knocked out against the sides of the narrow excavation if we moved, we came at last upon the hewers at work. There were two of them at the place lying naked in an oblique position, working at the face of the coal by hewing it down with picks – a pair of pitmen labouring thus are called marrows!**

We were shown the operation of blasting; a deep hole is bored into the coal, down which a quantity of gun powder in paper is driven, and a slow match is then made with a straw. Being lighted, we retired a short distance, and lay down to await the explosion, which thundered along the passage with grand effect. A vast quantity of coal was thus brought loose and broken with hammers into lumps of a size that could be put into baskets, which the putter boys then carried away. As a memento of our visit we lay down and hewed a small piece of coal and stored it in our pocket.

Several parts of the mine having been explored, we returned to the coup, feeling not the slightest envy of a pitman's life, for a man is not a 'moudiewort!'***

From the coup [tip], where the bare-legged putters were gathered together, we descended by means of the trams to the rolley-way, or high-street of this subterranean village, not particularly inclined to explore the labyrinthine alleys with which the coal field was intersected. It being time for part of the pitmen and boys to go home for the day, we were preceded and followed by a small procession of putters &c. with the 'dowps' [the ends] of their farthing candles stuck into clay held between their fingers. At intervals we passed a door, which is kept shut for ventilating purposes, except when trams or miners pass.

A small boy, called a trapper, sits all day in the dark behind the door to open it, and it must be a miserable life to lead for nine-pence a day. We were shown some chalk drawings by one of the trappers on the back of the door, to which, through love of fame and glory, he had affixed his name, John Storey.

Although there is no fire-damp in Shilbottle pit, and therefore accidents from explosion are unknown, there is a great deal of trouble and expense incurred to keep it clear of water. In one part of the pit, nine men are employed at a hand pump and three more at another place at the crank or gin**** where the horses were toiling round and round in a most monotonous occupation.

We sat down on a swing seat and had a ride around the ring, then returned to the bottom of the pit shaft, where the pitmen, having dressed themselves in rough flannel, took hold of the chain and were drawn out of the pit in clusters. It was raining heavily at the bottom of the shaft when we slipped our leg through a bight (loop) in the dirty chain, and grasping the links rose grandly out into the day.

Views of the wall that surrounded the capped mineshaft of keepers pit before the farmland was restored. *Julia Tweedy collection*

---

*   Rolley way – An early name for the rails on which coal carts were transported.
**   Mates; in local dialect 'marras'
***   Mouldiewort; In 1860 dialect 'moudie' was a mole.
**** Gin – a pole or beam used to turn a central hoist, pump or mill, often horse driven.

The sun was shining gorgeously, and the reflected rays on the white fields of snow offered a strong contrast to the darkness we had left behind, as does the change from an Indian temperature to that of a Scottish mountain in January. Resuming our garments at the pit mouth we walked off to the village to get the coaly stains washed from our faces and hands.

Coal from the cutting face was raised on sledges drawn from the face by men and boys, some as young as ten. During this period workings from the Keeper's Pit broke into very old 'bell-pit' workings in the vicinity of Greenrigg Kennels.

The shaft was very close to the Keeper's cottage adjacent to the road. The cottage's last residents were the Hood family. It was demolished and the mineshaft filled in, the land being restored for farming.

The Second Edition 6" to the mile Ordnance Survey map, c. 1897 shows old coal workings to the west of Colliery Farm and an old shaft south of the Old Coal Workshops. In addition the old shaft north of North Side is visible as is the old shaft at Shilbottle Old Pit, known as the Keepers.

In the centre of Shilbottle village was Town Pit which also had a 10 foot shaft diameter shaft. The pit had shallow seams 6 inches thick at 171 feet and 252 feet and half this height in a seam 271 feet below the surface. The Town Pit was sunk in 1844. It was located in Scott's 'Half-Acre', 100 yards north-west of the footpath from St. James' Church where it joins North Side.

East Pit, at the precise reference for Keeper's Pit on the 1897 map was sunk on 14th October, 1845 to a

Longdyke Colliery, taken from the west, the miners' houses in the Long Row visible in the background.

depth of 298 feet 5 inches. It was also known as Engine Pit or New Engine Pit. Small, unworkable seams were located at 173 feet and at 258 feet. However, the primary Shilbottle Seam at 285 feet was found to have 2 feet 4 inches of good quality coal.

Longdyke Colliery

Following long periods of consultation and feasibility studies including an assessment of the viability of extracting coal from a colliery at Bilton Banks, in 1796 the Duke of Northumberland issued an amended 21 year lease to allow Sir Geoffrey Cooper of Bilton and Bilton Banks to develop a mine at Longdyke. The legend on plans accompanying the lease indicates that a seam of 'whole coal' south of the Sandstone Dyke remained to be extracted.

In 1817 Thomas and Hugh Taylor held the lease for Shilbottle Colliery, then situated at Colliery Farm. 22nd August 1844 saw sinking start for Longdyke Pit. The Taylor brothers were still lessees of Shilbottle Colliery in 1860. However, around this time the ownership of the colliery at Longdyke passed from Sir Geoffrey Cooper to Henry Augustus Paynter, an Alnwick solicitor and his colleague solicitor Mr Nathaniel Dunn of Bedlington.

By 1867 the mine workings at Longdyke were initially 'bord and pillar', subsequently becoming long-wall. Eventually underground workings from Longdyke covered

Long Row facing onto the road, with one house from the Short Row just visible behind

2,221 acres and during the 23 years since its sinking, 3.5 million tons of coal had been raised. An estimated 5 million tons remained to be extracted.

On 27th March 1870, the Duke of Northumberland issued a 31 year lease on Shilbottle Colliery at Longdyke which included provision for a manager's house and 26 workmen's cottages.

> Women played a crucial role in all mining villages. They turned houses into homes, survived births or not, oversaw childhood ailments and guided teenagers through their most difficult years. They often became the principal carers for aged parents whilst their men-folk laboured underground or slept to refresh themselves for their next shift. The whole family had to be guided and often protected from the worst effects of the monstrous cruelty of an industry which was brutal and mostly uncaring of its workforce. Bread had to be baked, meals made ready for hungry labourers returning home, pit clothes had to be laundered, kettles boiled and tin baths made ready before the living room fire. Beyond the home, chapels had to be built and communities kept going in good times and bad.'*

The Long Row of houses at Bilton Banks were built of random and shaped stones. The Short Row was built of bricks. The image on the left above is of the rarely used front entrance of the west end house of the Short Row, occupied at the time by the Baxter family. The second image on the right is also of the Short Row.

Mr Ronnie Knox, interviewed by Vera Mallon for her Bailiffgate Museum article, said,

> Some of the women used to help each other out at special or difficult times for example when a baby was born or someone needed nursing, even laying out the dead. It was what people did in those days in close knit communities.
> Water was carried by the bucketful from a pump below the short row, and light was provided by paraffin lamps ... a tanker came to each house and dispensed the paraffin into whatever kind of receptacle was available.

Doreen Ions lived with her parents and three sisters at Bilton Banks.

> The house had two bedrooms upstairs and a large kitchen downstairs with a small scullery behind with a walk-in pantry where food could be kept cold. The kitchen was always warm ... we had a good supply of coal which was part of the miner's wages. The fire was banked up at night with ashes in the winter to keep it on until morning.
> The cast iron stove had a boiler for water on one side and an oven on the other. A pan rest would be swung over the fire when pans were needed for cooking and swung back when cooking was finished.
> We didn't have a bathroom so had to bathe in front of the kitchen fire.

The visitation, subject of the 1892 article on the *Northumberland Miner at Home*, summarised by Vera Mallon, referred to earlier, spoke of the village of Bilton and particularly the miners' homes:

> The pit village is an unattractive place, even when seen under the influence of fine weather and sunshine. Towering above everything ... arise the great ugly buildings connected to the engine and shaft, the various sheds, stables, storehouses and forges. The pit houses – entered immediately into a front room

Mrs Tweedy outside her Percy Road home, keeping up expected high standards. *Julia Tweedy collection*

---

* Margaret Hedley's *Women of the Durham Coalfields in the 19th century* published by History Press provides a relevant and touching insight into the role of women in mining villages in the county adjacent to Northumberland.

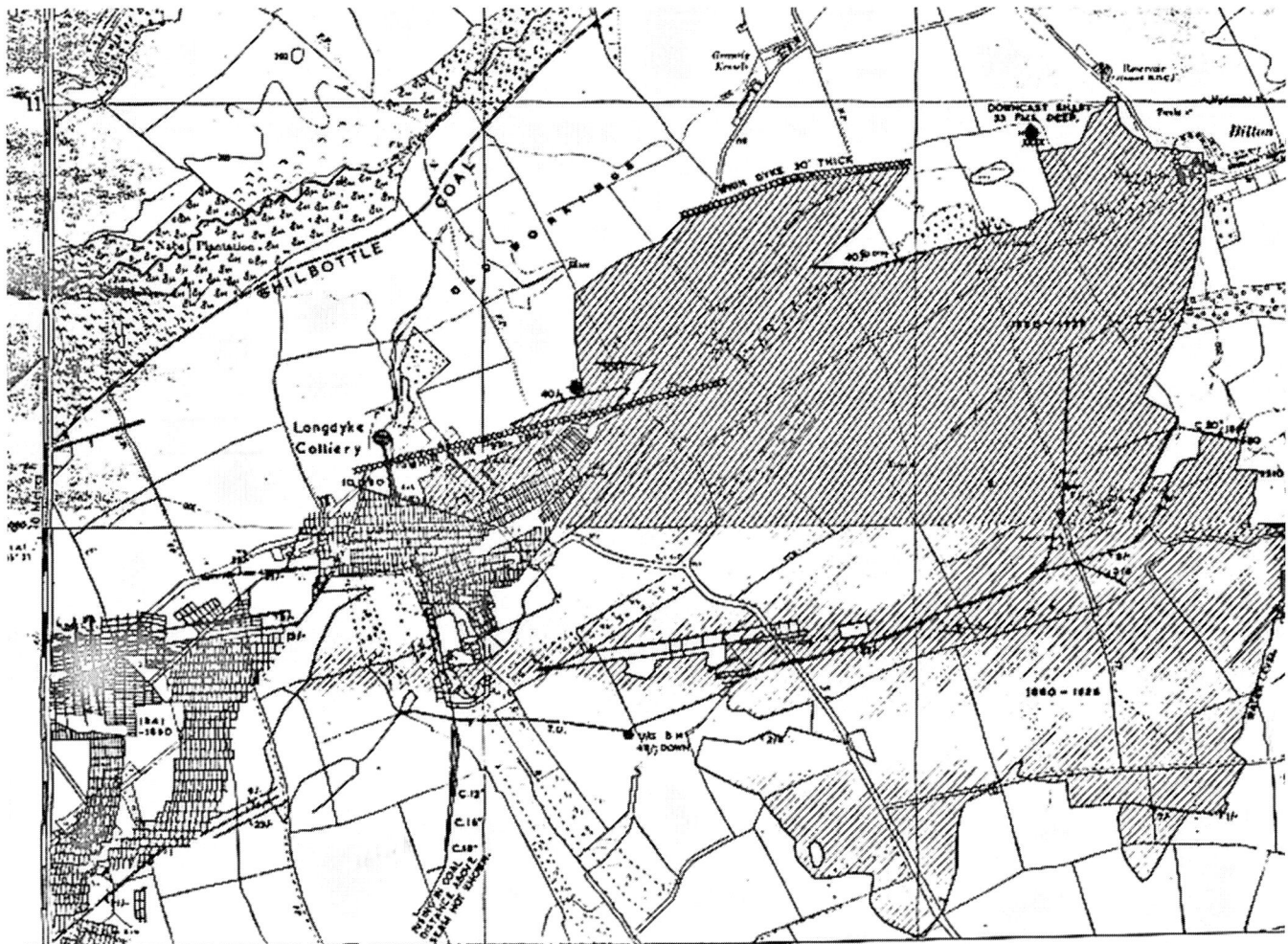

Map of the extent of underground longwall workings at Longdyke and the more primitive method of bord and pillar working with the darker squared marking.
Reproduced with permission of Northumberland Archive.

... is the massive splendour of the much be-brassed iron bed, for the most part hung in white and covered with gay striped cotton quilt. Here too is the mighty mahogany chest of drawers ... a couch, a chair covered in American leather, a coffin-cased eight-day clock, an ample circular table and several Wycombe wooden chairs ... and the civilising influence of a piano or American organ or other musical appliance ... the floor laid over with oil cloth and reposing in luxury in front of the glowing fire is a 'clouty' hearth rug in which can be picked out by an old acquaintance the remains of garments worn for years back by members of the household.

Despite the negative images painted of the village, research among previous householders of the village of Bilton Banks, may have understood the deprivation in which their homes were situated but they mostly loved living in community there.

The colliery at Longdyke was undoubtedly a profitable mining concern and in the 1880s a limited share release was offered, up to £30,000 and the Shilbottle Coal Company came into being.

Bord and pillar was used prior to 1880 and followed the practice of extracting coal around a pillar to leave a lattice-work of coal between bords to support the roof. Between 1880 and 1925 the longwall process was used and this was alternatively known as the 'total extraction' method, using two roadways or gates driven at fixed intervals, usual 100, 200 or 250 yards, depending on the roof's condition and the existence of faults in the surrounding stone. Total extraction, where this was possible, was completed between the two roadways or gates as the workers advanced. At Longdyke, the coalface was ventilated by the passage of air down the main gate along the coalface and out of the tail gate. The main gate was often known as the 'mother gate' because it fed air towards the face.

The down-cast shaft at Longdyke went to 320 feet and was located west of Bilton at the very edge of the coalfield. For a more comprehensive account of Longdyke Colliery see my book *Bilton Banks: The Pit and its People*.

In 1916 Longdyke Colliery at Bilton Banks passed into the ownership of the Co-operative Wholesale Society. It continued producing coal until 19th August, 1925 when it closed.

THE

SHILBOTTLE COLLIERS,

A DESCRIPTIVE SONG.

Sung by them when Sword-dancing, 1823.

[TUNE—THE KEEL-ROW.]

As you go through Shilbottle,
Shilbottle, Shilbottle,
As you go through Shilbottle,
You'll hear the Lasses sing,
Weel may the Pit work,
The Pit work, the Pit work;
Weel may the Pit work,
Our Bonny Lads are in.

There's Collier Lads at Acklington,
Likewise at Framlington,
About Broom-hill, and Newton,
Some Folks will make a ding;
But from Shilbottle are we,
And hope you'll all agree,
To join our merry glee,
And with us loudly sing.

CHORUS.
Weel may the Pit work,
The Pit work, the Pit work;
Weel may the Pit work,
We earn our money in.

The first we bring for you to scan
He's our canny Overman,
Who each morning weel does plan,
The work ere we begin;
Every hewer gives a score,
Each tram puts as much more,
Little Trapper to your door,
And at pay-night we'll sing
Weel may the Pit work, &c.

The Hewer doffs his Jacket,
And lowly on his cracket,
With might and main he's at it,
Swiftly his pick does fling;
He curves and nicks so nicely,
And drills and stems so tightly,
Then fires his shot off sprightly,
Which makes the roof to ring,
Weel may the Pit work, &c.

The putter now is plying;
With tram that's almost flying,
Every coal that's lying,
Unto the * Coup to bring;
Into each board and Jinking,
He gives a blink in,
'Long the Barraway clinking,
Still blithly does he sing,
Weel may the Pit work, &c.

Past each nook and siding
The Rollies they go gliding,
The Corf's so quickly riding,
You'd fancy it had wings;
By Banksman now its seized,
If small and slack he's teazed,
But round and full he's pleased,
And cheerily then he sings
Weel may the Pit work, &c.

The Coals now, without delay,
Carts are ready to convey,
Or, may be down the Waggon-way,
For Alnwick and its king;
But lest you think us prosing
We'd best with thanks be closing,
We would not set you dosing,
For 'tis you that make us sing,

Weel may the Pit work,
The Pit work, the Pit work,
Weel may the Pit work,
We earn our money in.

* Coup or Crane where the putter's charge ends.

Davison, Printer, Alnwick.

REGULATIONS

FOR CONDUCTING

SHILBOTTLE COLLIERY BOYS' SCHOOL.

I. THAT all the Boys employed in the Pit and about the concern, have the privilege of attending this School, which shall be open two Evenings in each week, viz. *TUESDAY* and *THURSDAY*, from 5 until 8 o'Clock, between the 1st of October and the 31st of March.

II. There shall be taught Reading, Writing, and the lower branches of Arithmetic.

III. The Master shall be wholly paid by the Colliery tenants, who will also, in the first instance, provide requisite books, copies, &c.

IV. Besides the attendance on these week evenings, the Boys shall meet in the School every Sunday morning throughout the year, precisely at half after 9 o'Clock, when the psalms for the day shall be read over, as also the Epistle and Gospel; the master teaching how to find the different parts of the service, and to make the proper responses, which shall be done aloud; the whole of the boys proceeding, when the bell rings, to Church, headed by the master.

V. It being most proper and necessary that each boy should have a Bible and Prayer-Book of his own, a payment of 3d. per week shall be made by each, to be applied to the purchasing of these books, and when they are obtained, the subscription to be reduced to one penny per week, to assist in buying School books, paper, &c.

VI. A book to be provided, wherein the name of each Scholar shall be entered, and an exact account kept of their attendance, with any remarks on their individual progress and conduct that the master may deem requisite; such book to be regularly inspected by the Lessees when at the Colliery, or in their absence, whom they shall appoint; that in case of not attending regularly, or bad behaviour, the offending boy may be admonished, and should he not attend and behave better, he must, for the sake of example, suffer the disgrace of expulsion from the School.

VII. It would be very desirable, and is particularly requested by the Colliery tenants, that by way of giving countenance and encouragement to the boys, their fathers or friends should attend the School on the Sabbath mornings.

[Printed by W. DAVISON, Alnwick.]

Shilbottle Colliers Song and Colliery Boys School Regulations.

Reproduced with permission of Northumberland Archive.

The Shilbottle Colliers Descriptive Song of 1823

Being a miner was a dangerous occupation. Despite this, the pit men seemed to make light of their work as the Shilbottle Colliers' Song of 1823 seems to imply.

Shilbottle Colliery Boys' School

Boys employed in the collieries were offered basic education. The regulations from the 1820s, shown above, for the Shilbottle Colliery Boys' School, set out the conditions they were obliged to meet.

John Buddle the much respected mining engineer, more commonly called Colliery Viewer in the 19th century, speaking in 1842 of a hereditary working class and particularly the employment of boys as young as ten as coal miners, said, 'Our peculiar race of pitmen ... can only be kept up by breeding ... it could never be recruited from an adult population.'* So far as Shilbottle was concerned, he was so right. Most boys followed their fathers into mining.

Miners' Hostel

In the 1920s the owners of Shilbottle, Whittle and Longframlington Collieries used Swarland Old Hall as a 'miners' hostel,' to accommodate some of the workforce for their three collieries whilst the necessary housing was being built.**

Fatalities at Longdyke Colliery

The potential for injury was taken seriously as was training in mine rescue and first aid.

The Durham Mining Museum lists the following incomplete details of men and boys who were killed at Longdyke between 1881 and 1823:31

Name	Age	Date of death	Cause
J. Wrigglesworth	40	1st Apr 1881	Fall of stone
Frederick Weightman	14	17th Jun 1881	Fall of stone
Charles Taylor	44	29th Jan 1892	Explosion
Thomas Ternent	54	9th Dec 1901	Fall of stone

* Evans, Richard, *The Pursuit of Power*, Europe 1815 -1914, (U.K. Penguin Books, Random House) 2016, p 165.

** From a research article entitle 'Borderlands' by Rt Rev Stephen Platten, published in the *Berwick Advertiser and Berwickshire News* on 27th June 2019 p. 19.

A first aid training day, taken outside the Church of England school at Shilbottle in 1908.30
Standing left to right: Temple Wilson (Powder Magazine Manager and First Aid attendant), Tom Baxter, Fore-Overman, R. Henderson (Deputy), Unknown, W. Storey (Depot Attendant, Alnwick), Mr Kennedy (Depot Manager, Alnwick), Unknown, W. Dixon, (Electrician), Ed Dixon, (Back-Overman), Unknown, Unknown, Jack Scott (Overman and later under Manager).
Sitting left to right: Coverdale S Anderson (Electrician and later Under Manager then Manager), M. Storey, (Under Manager), Reverend Percy T Lee (Vicar Shilbottle), J.A. Storey (Manager – retired 1928), Edwin Anderson, (Stores Attendant & Local Preacher), J.H. Henderson, Deputy, R.G. Weightman (Deputy).

Reproduced with permission of Northumberland Archives NRO 1426 -02

George Foster/Selby	39	18th Jun 1905	Fall of stone
Thomas Newton	26	16th Jun 1906	Fall of stone
John Storey	25	19th Apr 1911	Fall of stone
William Taylor	60	21st Jan 1915	Crushed by tubs
John Shell	16	26th Sep 1916	Crush injury.
Martin Ryan	28	24th Oct 1917	Fall of stone
William Rogers Pringle	20	17th Jun 1920	Pneumonia.*
James Skinner	32	24th Jan 1921	Entangled
William Alexander Mitcheson	48	7th Aug 1922	Fall of stone
J. Ternent	44	26th Mar 1923	Gas explosion
Lancelot Wilkinson Chicken	46	28th Apr 1925	Fall of stone

The Northumberland Coal Owners Mutual Protection Association's records provide details (except in two cases) of the circumstances leading to the fatalities.

The registers, which run to nine, 6 inch thick volumes of records and minutes of the 'Association,' provide tangible proof of the hazards of coal mining. The index alone, with single spaced, typed entries is an inch thick. Each line in the book provides a statistic and marks the loss of a life, or serious injury through industrial accident, giving rise to a claim for compensation.

It is probable that there would have been more accidents involving injury than those recorded because the work was hard and physically demanding, requiring risk taking, ingenuity, strength of purpose and brute force, sometimes in the most hostile of environments.

Shilbottle Grange Colliery

The sinking of Shilbottle Grange pit commenced in 1921 and was completed in 1925. It was sunk between two geological faults which had bounded Longdyke's workings on the south side and another believed to be approximately 300 feet rising south. This ran in an east and west direction under Sturton Grange and was on the north side of workings in the Whittle Pit which had been worked from the outcrop of the seam. The north boundary of the workings at Shilbottle was the Whin Dyke in the area of Selby Stead which persisted eastwards in a line below Woodhouse Farm.

---

* Listed by Durham Mining Museum – but death considered by Coroner's Jury to be not related to an injury three years previously.

Shilbottle Grange Colliery

Shilbottle Colliery – a view taken from the west.

The colliery offices, pit-head baths and caretaker's house. *Ken Middlemist collection*

The then owners of the pit, namely the CWS, concluded prior to 1946, that the geological conditions being met underground by the colliers were likely to prevent the easy and financially viable 'winning' of coal using Shilbottle's shaft as the entry points. At this time the CWS had also taken over the South Shilbottle Company's Whittle Pit. They also had the Royalty rights south of the 300 feet fault at Sturton Grange. It was therefore decided to drive a drift through the fault to work the very large areas of coal in the Shilbottle seam. The drift started in 1946 and reached coal in 1947, when a second drift was driven at a very steep gradient for a return airway.

In 1946, under plans agreed by the Ministry of Fuel and Power, and later adapted under the National Coal Board, a 12 foot by 10 foot locomotive drift was driven out approximately 1 mile from the south shaft bottom to reach the coal at the south side of Sturton Grange fault. Mine cars with 2.25 tons capacity replaced the traditional 7.5 cwt tubs. Haulage powered by electricity, replaced main and tailgate haulers. In 1961 the NCB developed Whittle Colliery by driving a new surface drift allowing both collieries to increase coal output per day to 2500 tons.

The Details

The sinking of Shilbottle Grange Pit and Coal Production.

The first coal produced at Shilbottle Grange Pit was in 1926.

During the sinking of the shafts, 89 men were employed on the surface and 38 in the shaft or underground. Meanwhile Longdyke had 267 men and boys employed underground and 98 on the surface.

The lower left image shows the western aspect of Shilbottle Grange Colliery's surface offices. The stone building near the centre, opposite

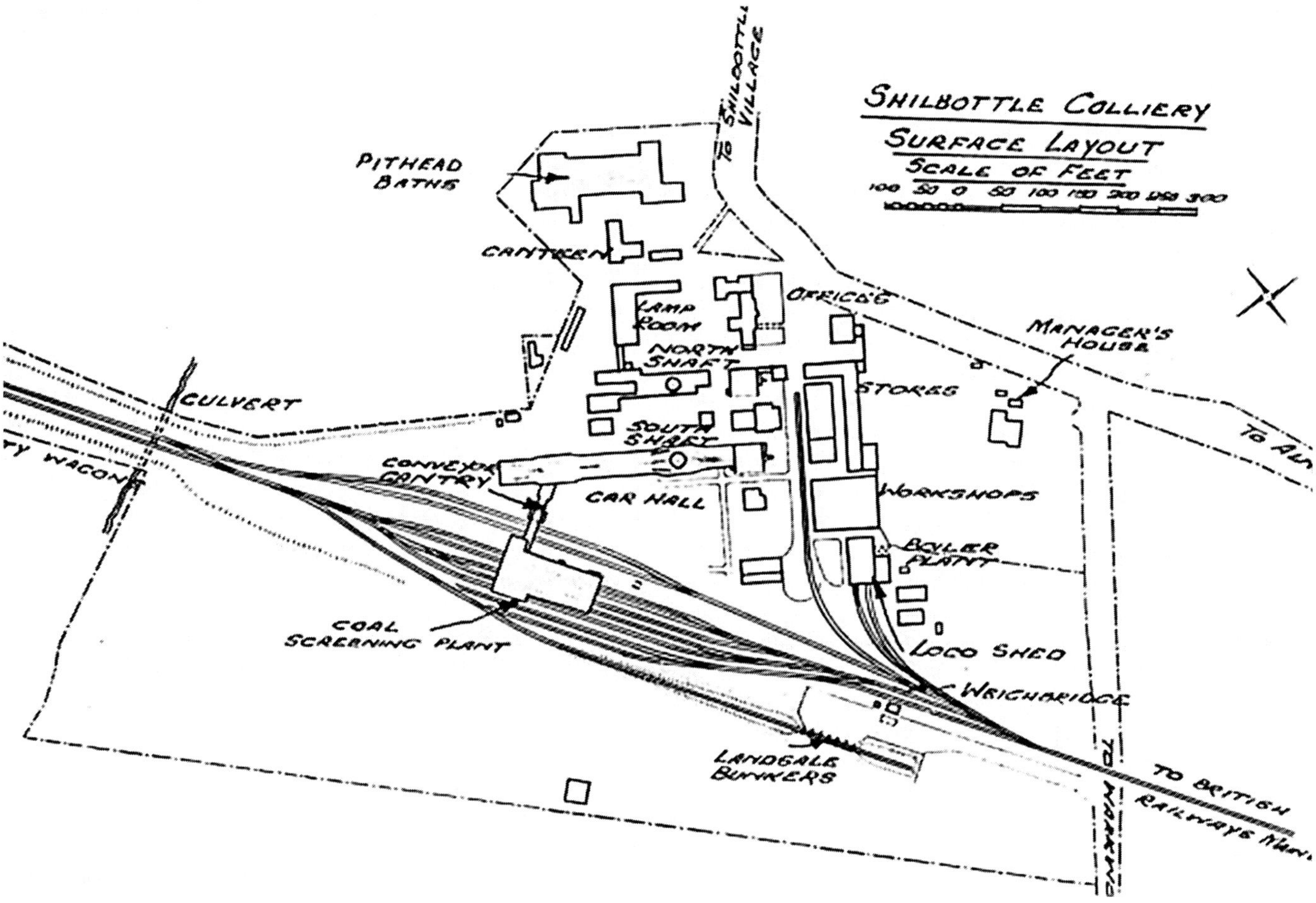

Architect's drawing of the surface complex of Shilbottle Colliery. *Terry Wayman collection*

the triangle of gardens, was the baths superintendent/caretaker's house. The left portion of the stone building was the manager's office. The under-manager and colliery officials had their office on the right side of the lawn. The pit-head baths, rescue office/first aid room and canteen were to the right. The pit-head winding gear for the north shaft is on the left edge of the photograph.

For 60 or more years the colliery buildings at Shilbottle Grange were a constant reminder of an industry which provided the fuel for steel making, munitions during two wars, gas and electricity power supply and of course great profit for the nation. The surface buildings were visible on the approach roads from Warkworth and when leaving the village to travel west down the steep slope leading to Woodhouse farm and beyond.

The winding gear, for both shafts were 'Roben' make and each were exact duplicates. Each shaft was 16 feet in diameter and both were lined with pre-cast concrete blocks. The shaft capacity was 42 tons per hour and the winding plant was designed to take a double cage, bringing the output to 65 tons per hour or 910 tons per 14 hour day. The South shaft was the 'Upcast' shaft; the North: a coal drawing shaft. Both were 945 feet deep.

The Colliery yard, workshops and 'Tankie' yard looking south taken from a position east of the manager's house.

---

*   Robey A.C. reduction geared 12.5 to 1, 300 HP, 2750 Volts, cylindrical drum, Metrovick motors.

The 'sinkers' for Shilbottle's new pit were initially housed in the former Army huts erected east of what became Garden Terrace, in Shilbottle Grange. 'Children of the sinkers swamped the school in Shilbottle village. Consequently, children from the colliery houses at Bilton were transferred to Lesbury School.'* The first sods cut for the shaft, under the supervision of Ned Dixon, manager of Longdyke, were witnessed by local people.** One of the first sinkers*** came from Egremont at the invitation of the principal sinker Mr Johnson.**** Mr Johnson said that when the work of sinking began, 'the two imposing headgears for winding up the debris' were already erected

Mr Johnson

Nearby were the screens, constructed of steel and brickwork with concrete floor with sufficient clearance to take 40 ton wagons. The screens had four belts to take best coal, cobbles, and smalls.† The belts and loading were all powered by electricity. 'Nearby was a blacksmiths' fitting shops, engine houses and in the distance, a new village was in the process of being built.' Mr Johnson later lodged in this estate with Mr and Mrs McLean at 33 Colliers Close.†† *Sinking work started at 6 am and went on around the clock, blasting, drilling and shovelling as the shaft descended at the rate of about 5 feet per day. The conditions were always wet.*

The local men involved in the sinking included Harry Moorhead, Billy Dixon the engineer, and Jack Taylor with his team including Joe Parkinson and John Levetti. One hundred men were involved in the enterprise.

When Longdyke closed in 1925, the workforce transferred to the Grange Pit. In 1925 the Grange Pit employed 320 men and boys underground and 158 on the surface. Over the decades, up to 1947, when the National Coal Board took ownership of Shilbottle Grange Pit from the Co-operative Wholesale Society, the number of underground miners rose to 370 and surface workers reduced to 130.

The colliery extracted coal using 60, 80 and 100 yard hand-filling faces, moving the coal underground, initially using pit ponies and endless and main-tail rope haulage. Underground ventilation was achieved through two 54" 'Sirocco' Fans, each working in parallel, driven by two 20 H.P. A.C. induction motors. The colliery's power of 20,000 volts was purchased from N.E.E.S. Company. This was transformed by three 'in-bye' transformers to 2,750 volts, and 650 volts. The lighting transformer reduced the voltage to 110 volts.

Initially the colliery had two Saddle Tank locomotives to take the loaded coal wagons along the

The headgesr of Shilbottle Colliery.   *Davy Dunn collection*

Shilbottle's 'fitters' with Mr Jack Jobson, Engineer, 3rd from the left.
Maureen Winn (née Jobson) collection

---

*   Extracted from a note written by John Stewart in 1970.
**   Conversations between Judith Line, Jean Hall and Lilian Hume in February and May 2017.
***   This gentleman was Mrs Jean Hall's grandfather (Jean a long-time resident of Shilbottle and a source of much information).
**** The image taken from a *Journal* article of Monday 15th March 1982) and reproduced with permission.
†   Best coal 4½ inches and over; cobbles 2½ inches to 4½ inches; smalls 1¼ inches.
††   A hand-drawn map prepared by Robert Tate in April 1817 for Earl Percy (Northumberland Castle, Archives Ref AC/O: V1 13) shows a field between Greenrigg and Bilton named 'Colliers' Close'.

two miles of private railway to the LNER line at Lane House Sidings, south of Alnmouth Station. Each trip handled around 180 tons of coal.

Following Nationalisation, between 1948 and 1952 an underground, three mile, straight roadway for locomotives, was driven to allow the mine to work on the 'horizon' mining system. All the coal was taken to a single loading point and from there transported to the shafts. During this transition, the two shafts were reversed. The old up-cast shaft became the coal-drawing shaft and the old North, coal shaft, became the ventilation shaft. Shilbottle used locomotives to transport its coal. At its peak in 1951 Shilbottle produced 272,000 tons of coal per year and employed 832 men, 648 underground.

What was mining like?

In his unpublished memoirs, John Stewart, *The life and times of John Stewart* (1995), he provides interesting details about his work at Shibottle Colliery. He started there eight years after the colliery opened, on 7th August 1933, a week after his 14th birthday.

John Stewart (known mostly as Johnnie at the pit, Jack by his wife) at Shilbottle Colliery in 1960.

On arrival at the colliery on a visit with father the day I left school, I was surprised – the pit yard area appeared to be like an elaborate and organised junk yard with tubs and other pieces of equipment standing and lying about all over the place. The shaft accommodated two cages, each capable of holding three tubs or 18 men. When one cage was at the top the other was at the bottom and they were counter-balanced to pass midway in the shaft. The up shaft was also the route by which fresh air was drawn into the mine. When we arrived at the bottom of the shaft I was surprised to find the whole area so well lit with fitted electric lights and with brick walls so clean and whitewashed.*

These conditions existed for only a few yards on each side of the shaft bottom and extreme darkness was the state of things beyond. The most vivid recollection is of the smell ... a mixture of thick black grease ... pit water in the sump, mud and old wood.

Two weeks later his proper shift started.

Full tubs were coming out of the pit and running towards the screens for the coal to be cleaned and graded. Empty tubs were clanking their way back from the screens towards the pit top. Steam locomotives were shunting railway wagons under the screens where they were being loaded for delivery to the main line railway stations ... Men were hurrying about and altogether there was an atmosphere of interest and urgency.

At the bottom of the shaft,

the noise was absolutely deafening ... the racket of steel ropes running over rollers and pulleys, the clatter of tubs, the roar of huge haulage situated 50 yards to the rear, the swish of cage ropes and the clank of chains as the cages arrived. Conversation was impossible and most instructions were given by hand signals.

At the bottom of the shaft John Stewart was employed as 'on-setter', supervising the entry into the cage of three tubs full of coal and the uncoupling of three empty tubs as they were shunted out by the full ones. The empty tubs were attached to an endless rope and sent, in a line of 34, to the face for refilling. He worked 'foreshift', beginning at 2 am and backshift (or dayshift) beginning at 10 am, on alternate weeks. He progressed after about 11 months to working 'in-bye' in the Seventh North district of the pit. His role was to supervise the 'flat' or collecting point for the tubs brought from the coal face, to couple the tubs and use a 10 HP direct hauler** to bring, and then assemble, the empty tubs for their return to the coal face for refilling. By the time he was 16 years old he was being offered occasional piece work, earning twice as much as his father who, as an injured war veteran, worked on the screens. John Stewart went home with a weekly wage of 12s. 6d. As a 17 year old he was upgraded to be a putter's helper; his duties then were to deliver empty tubs to the 'fillers' and remove the filled ones. On one occasion he refers to a fire damp explosion which sent flame rushing towards him, his escape from serious burns being managed by his squeezing himself flat to the floor. Later he broke a wrist when attempting to stop a run-away tub.

In the first year he wore out eleven pairs of trousers and six pairs of boots. In 1954, aged 35 years, John Stewart was appointed overman at the colliery.

After qualifying by examination in 1962 to be a colliery manager, he left Shilbottle for Ellington Colliery where he was appointed senior overman/relief under-manager. A year later he was appointed under-manager at Lynemouth Colliery.

Writing about a fatal accident in the colliery, claiming the lives of three men, on 14th May 1940, John Stewart explained some of the working practices of the mine.

In 1940, Shilbottle Colliery was a mixture of the old and the then new. The colliery began working in February 1925, and was sited (sic) on a farm known as Shilbottle Woodhouse. The rights to working the coal had been purchased by the Cooperative Wholesale Society for £50.00. The two shafts were

---

* A report written on 17th March 1926 for the Co-operative Wholesale Society (NRO1758) confirms John Stewart's recollection, stating that 'the shaft bottom resembles an underground subway, being substantially bricked throughout.

** These were auxiliary electricity driven haulers which superseded ponies.

almost 1000 feet deep (960 feet to be exact) if the water sump was included. When work first began at the mine, all the coal was 'hand got' in the 28 inch seam, which was the only seam being worked. This means that men known as hewers used hand held picks and hewed the bottom of the seam out as far as they could reach. This operation was continued across the whole of their 'stint' – usually 10 yards – with the seam being 'chocked' up as they progressed.

On completion of the 'kinving' as it was known, one shot-hole was then drilled to the same depth as the undercut. This was loaded with a suitable amount of gunpowder, formed into 'bobbins', so called because they resembled cotton reels. The shot-hole was stemmed, using a pricker (to ensure there was a clear passage to the powder) and a beater, to tamp in the stemming material. This material was usually only loose dirt or rubbish which was lying around. Then a squib – rather like a straw filled with loose powder, was inserted. The workman then lit the squib and retired to a safe distance. Sparks from the squib, travelled along the small, channel left by the 'pricker' until they reached the main charge. The resultant blast allowed the coal to be got by pick and shovel and filled into tubs. These metal tubs held approximately 7cwts of coal. They had a staple to which was attached the respective 'tallies' of the man who filled the tub, and the putter who was responsible for getting the tub in and out of the working place.

Until 1937 the colliery was completely a 'naked light' mine. This means that all the workmen used either hand held flame lamps or smaller cap lamps. In the early days, these were oil fuelled and for good reason, were called 'smokies' or 'midgies'. Later, acetylene lamps became the recognised form of lighting.

Fillers or hewers, stone-men and people whose workplace

The man-riding cage at the shaft bottom at Shilbottle. *Davy Dunn collection*

was fairly static, used the larger hand held lamp. These were furnished with a big hook which could be affixed to a nearby prop or ledge. Workers who needed to be more mobile, like putters or general datal hands, used the smaller brass cap lamp.

Ignitions of accumulations of flammable gas were fairly frequent. These were usually small incidents and many never came to notice of the colliery management. About 1930, coal-cutting machines were introduced and these eliminated the need for hand hewing in a general sense. Occasionally, for specific reasons, a man would be given the task of hewing in a special location. The skills of hewing were thus often still required.

Coal cutting machines cut along the seam at floor level, to a depth of 4 feet 6 inches.

Two men operated the electrically powered machines and the cutting was normally done in the nightshift, commencing about 2 hours after the stone-men had begun their work.

It should be noted that while all workmen used naked flame lamps, officials carried safety lamps to allow tests to be made at regular intervals and in likely places. When coal cutting machines became the order of the day, a working district or 'flat', consisted of 10 'places.' These were parallel to each other and 10 yards apart – 5 on the rise side, one (the main gate or mother gate) straight ahead, and 4 on the dip side. The seam inclined about 1 in 10, dipping north-east to south-west, but roadways serving each working place were kept as near level as possible. This was to facilitate getting tubs in and out to fillers. This work being done by piece workers, known as putters, each of whom, while working as an individual was provided with a 'helper.' This helper was paid by the company but where conditions allowed, was 'tipped' by his putter at the

The shaft bottom at Shilbottle believed to be in the 1970s. The larger coal 2.25 ton capacity tubs provide the clue. *Davy Dunn collection*

Workings in a 27 inch seam towards the coal face at Shilbottle.

Davy Dunn collection

end of the week. These workers travelled from a putters' flat, where full and empty tubs were accumulated, before being taken either in or out. From the putters flat 'in bye' (inwards towards the face) roadways were about 5 feet 6 inches wide and no more than 5 feet high, but often settled to a much lower height. Many times barely high enough to allow a tub to pass. The putters' flat was double sided with empty tubs being collected on one side and full ones delivered to the other. The numbers varied according to conditions and circumstances, but could be anything from 7 to 17. If 17 empties were sent in from 'out-bye' (shaftwards) then 17 full tubs had to be returned. There was a limit to what any putters' flat could accommodate. No flat was really typical but there was a recognised pattern of working. This was a form of 'longwall' mining which was later adapted to suit conveyor working when these were installed in about 1941. Each flat was controlled in each shift, by an official, a Deputy overman, although for some reason the nightshift deputy was always called a 'chargeman.' These officials were responsible for all operations and particularly to enforce safety regulations and the Coal Mines Act.

The coal cutting machine would travel in one direction during one cut and in the opposite direction for the next. Sometimes exceptional circumstances prevented this system from working and alternative arrangements had to be made. Often these were made by a deputy without consultation with his superior – an 'Overman'.

Before the installation of conveyors and even for a short time afterwards a recognised system for the fair allocation of work was in vogue at Shilbottle. This was the 'cavilling system' and was largely a matter of luck rather like a lottery. The names of fillers, putters and 'stonemen' were drawn out of a container, and so for 12 or 14 weeks a man knew where he was to work. This was for good or bad and as it was all piece work, the man's standard of living was so controlled for the ensuing quarter of the year.

Coal cutter men who were responsible for their machines were exempt from the cavils and stayed in a district until it finished. The fillers worked in teams of 4 men and stonemen in sets of 2. Usually they were members of the same family and often good friends. The choice was their own as to whom they worked with, but the various sets had to ensure their names were in the hands of management and the union secretary before the cavils could be drawn. Putters were individual workers and had no 'marras.' The cavils were drawn in strict rotation to ensure, as far as possible, that they were absolutely fair. Each set of 4 fillers would be directed to 2 working places at the coal face, and each set of 2 stonemen (or counchmen) would also be given 2 places. Putters were cavilled according to the number of places on each district – and perhaps more important – the conditions which applied there. The cavils were drawn in a clockwise direction for both the mine as a whole and for each flat. Commencing with the district which was farthest away, on the dip-side of the shafts, the fillers were drawn first. The first fillers to be drawn would be the 4 men who would work the 2 bottom places of the lowest district. Two of the men would work the early shift while two would work the back shift, alternating each week. On each flat or district the men working the bottom places were the 'first cavillers' and as

Mr Billy Buddle and the late Mel Watson using an electrically powered coal cutting shearer at the Y65 coal face at Whittle.

Davy Dunn collection

Moving tubs by hand at Shilbottle Colliery.

such, in whatever circumstances, would have first claim on any work on the face in that district. Twenty fillers and 10 stonemen were needed to work the district. Three or four putters, with an appropriate number of helpers would be required to service the fillers. There were, of course, ancillary workers not mentioned. However, the 4 fillers would have priority for any coal filling in that district as would the 2 stonemen given the same places for any counch work. Occasionally extra men would need to be drafted into a district.

About every 100 or 150 yards a new rise and a new dip heading would need to be driven. This would depend on the inclination of the seam and roadways. Meanwhile, a new putters' flat would be prepared behind the new headings.

Piece work allowed men to increase earning by working a bit harder. At the same time there was a minimum wage of 6 shillings and 9½ pence per shift.

Shilbottle Colliery, during the times mentioned was looked upon as having the best conditions of employment in the country. It had a minimum wage and was the first colliery in Britain to allow its staff to have one week's paid holiday per year. Yet there were anomalies dating back to earlier days. The only tools provided to the men, who qualified for them, were a shovel and an axe. They had to buy the remainder of their tools. This included lamps and explosives and everything else required for their respective trades. In 1925 all colliers at Shilbottle were obliged to join a union affiliated to the Trades Union Congress. The union of choice was the National Union of Mineworkers.

In 1937 a small incident occurred in which a man was burnt. Management took the opportunity to recommend that workmen should buy electric safety cap lamps, instead of using acetylene (carbide gas) lamps. As with all tools, these could be purchased through the colliery, with weekly deductions from pay slips. As smoking underground was still permitted, it was difficult to convince workmen that these 'new fangled' electric lamps would be an advantage to them. The management of the mine were in a cleft stick too. They didn't want to insist on these lamps being used, or that explosive gas was being found fairly regularly. Otherwise, the colliery would have its classification changed to 'a safety lamp' mine. This would have meant that all explosives used in the mine would have to be of the so called 'safe', or permitted type. This would also have meant that only deputies would be authorised to fire shots, which would restrict the flexibility of shot firing. Until then, men could fire shots when these were needed. A change would mean that they would have to wait the availability of the deputy. Besides this, black powder (or gun powder) had been found to be the most suitable for the hard Shilbottle coal.

On May 14th 1940, when the fatal explosion occurred, many men were still using flame lamps and black powder. Strangely, permission to smoke underground had been withdrawn. To do so was deemed to be illegal. However, black powder shots were fired by the deputy using fuse and detonator. Shots using permitted explosive were fired by means of a cable and battery (generator) and electric detonators.

It was a time of confused priorities and instructions. Men were forbidden to smoke by law, yet allowed to carry a naked flame lamp. A 'filler' could carry both black powder and permitted explosive, with detonators for his black powder in a small box. Certain workmen had been nominated to carry flame safety lamps, in addition to their normal lamps for lighting purposes. One man in every 8, or less, had to carry one of these testing lamps for general safety purposes. All coal cutter-men had to have a testing lamp near the machine; haulage enginemen needed these lamps in their work places. Any men working alone or in isolated places were obliged to have a lamp nearby. Occasionally, the nominated lamp carrier was still using a naked flame lamp. All of this in a working situation where colliery management were refusing to admit that gas was being discovered on a regular basis.

A coal 'Tankie' leaving Shilbottle Colliery to connect with the main line south-east of High Buston.

Courtesy Roy Lambeth Durham Mining Museum

The 'Tankies' were war time Austerity locomotives built during the Second World War, some remained in service until 1973.
Courtesy Roy Lambeth
Durham Mining Museum

A 'Side Tipper' truck, mainly used for the carriage and disposal of stone drawn from the pit.
Courtesy Roy Lambeth
Durham Mining Museum

One of the 'tankies' reversed into the sidings (now a car park for walkers).
Courtesy Roy Lambeth
Durham Mining Museum

Crossing the Shilbottle road east of the manager's house.
*Courtesy Roy Lambeth
Durham Mining Museum*

'Tankie' seen at dusk from the Tylaw Burn, returning to the colliery after delivering a load to the main line.
*Courtesy Roy Lambeth
Durham Mining Museum*

Workmen outside the 'tankie' sheds at Shilbottle Colliery Andy Anderson (on the locomotive), and L-R, Ian Wallace, Selby Knox, Bob Douglas. *Davy Dunn collection*

Coal 'won' from Shilbottle Colliery.

Coal from the Shilbottle Seam was in constant demand by domestic and industrial consumers. Compared with coal from other collieries the residual ash was less than 4% as opposed to the average of 14%.

The output, of the sought after coal from Shilbottle, was delivered by rail and road to Tyneside and from the NCB's harbour at Amble by ship to the east coast of Scotland, the Scottish Isles and, by road, to the South Eastern Electricity Board.

In 1947 there were 543 workers at Shilbottle Colliery, 183 at the coal face. They were producing 390 tons of coal a day (108,296 a year) At the end of 1948 major restructuring was undertaken at the colliery, it then being estimated that it had a life of 100 years, there being coal reserves to provide an output of 309,600 tons per annum. The improvement scheme, completed over an 11 year period, cost £468,964. The scheme included better entrance roads for land-sale of coal, better paths, reconstructed workshops, storehouse, fan house, engine house, pit bottom 'drivages', locomotive drift and locomotive house.

The restructuring scheme included the abandonment of coal winding at the North Shaft and the equipping of the South Shaft for winding 2¼ ton capacity mine cars.

At the pit bottom of the South Shaft a 3 foot gauge rail track was laid complete with mine car control equipment. 'Drivage' equipment was installed for a distance of 1,500 yards. Conveyors and coal cutters for longwall faces were fitted and these were complemented by trunk conveyors to two-car loading stations at the end of the drift. Minerals, supplies and men were transported by 60H.P. Logan battery locomotives along the drift; and at the bottom of the shaft there was the engine house. Between 1957 and 1959 pithead baths with 72 showers, 18 of the open type were provided for the workforce of 810 men. A fully equipped medical treatment centre was added.

Pre 1947 – men at the North Shaft ready to descend into the pit. *Margery Slater collection*

The South Shaft with new equipment to handle 2¼ ton mine cars.

Three foot gauge railway at the pit bottom.

Colliers, following the receipt of their Long Service Awards at Shilbottle Colliery.
Back Row: William Anderson Willcox in the centre; two from the right William Egdell with Ned Donaldson on the extreme right.
Front Row: with his arms folded, Mr David Archbold (Regional Director) and next to him on the right, Shilbottle Colliery's manager Mr Stan Robson, Mr Buglass and Jimmy Wilson.
Kenneth Wilcox collection

Colliery representatives including Temple Wilson, Stan Weightman, Mark Swan, Tom Bell and Basil Ray, with Joe Ternent seated third left in Shilbottle Working Men's Club on 10th April 1976 with representatives of the C.W.S. Pensons Scheme.
Kieth Wilson collection

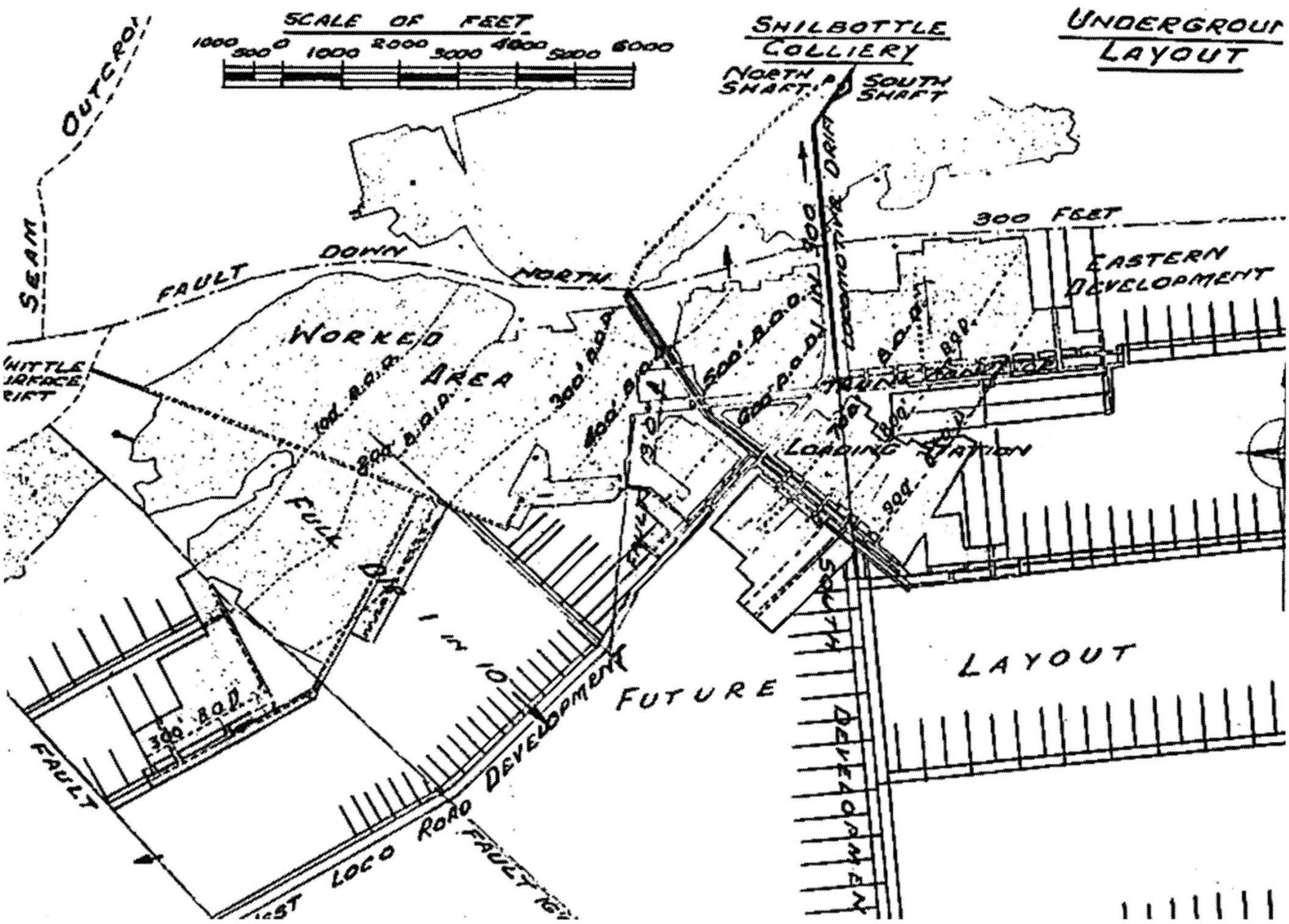

The underground layout of the colliery in the 1960s. *Terry Wayman collection*

By 1961, 796 men were employed at Shilbottle colliery; 286 at the coalface. Production had increased to 267,144 tons of coal per year.

The underground workings of extracted coal from Shilbottle and surrounding areas extended east beyond Bilton Mill, south across to Sturton Grange, beyond Whittle and Newton on the Moor in the south-west.

Shilbottle Colliery's nurse

Alma moved from Lancashire to the village in 1942 to be employed by Shilbottle Colliery as colliery nurse and midwife. She later worked for Northumberland County and travelled, as required, across Alnwick District as a community nurse. She married Joe Ternent, Shilbottle Colliery's Union Secretary. Their daughter Maureen was among a minority of pupils from the village school to receive a Grammar School education at the Duchess School in Alnwick.

The village's nurse was Annabelle Thompson, who lived in Grange Road. Her position pre-dated Alma's appointment by several years.

Alma Ternent. *Maureen Davis (née Ternent) collection*

Newton on the Moor Colliery

Newton on the Moor Colliery, also known as the Hunter Pit or Dyke Head, was sunk in 1835 to a depth of 317 feet to the Shilbottle seam which was 2 feet 9 inches thick. The lesser known Riddel Pit was 200 yards south. The owner of Hunter Pit from 1860 was Mr R.G. Reed and from 1880 Mr S.F. Widdrington. In 1890 ownership passed to Newton Coal Co Ltd (later Newton Colliery Co Ltd). Coal produced at the colliery was primarily for land sale and household use. In 1896 there were 28 employees, 24 of whom worked underground. In 1902 there were only 21 men and boys underground, also with four on the surface. The colliery was abandoned in 1889 when the coal was worked out or the 'winning of it' was compromised through flooding.

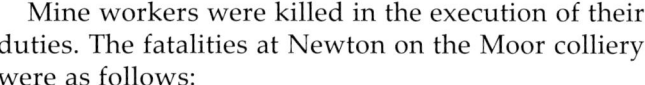

Newton on the Moor Colliery *Phil Huntley collection*

Mine workers were killed in the execution of their duties. The fatalities at Newton on the Moor colliery were as follows:

> **Robert Jenkinson Bennison**, (the manager's son and not usually employed at the colliery) aged 20 on 22nd August 1903. He was approximately 270 feet down the shaft assisting another man to fit an attachment to a suction pipe when he was hit by a falling stone and knocked into the water below where he drowned.
>
> **William Cowell**, aged 15 years was killed by a fall of stone on 6th February 1857.
>
> **John Purvis**, aged 30 years, a hewer was killed by a fall of timber from the shaft side.
>
> **William Richardson**, a fireman was killed by a boiler explosion on 17th July, 1862.
>
>> 'The boiler which caused the death of Mr Richardson, (and seriously injured a workman called Ramsey), ... was propelled ... from Newton Colliery a distance of 200 yards ... onto the turnpike road north of the pit mouth.' *Newcastle Guardian and Tyne Mercury*, 19th July, 1862
>
> **Thomas Riddell**, aged 67, a furnaceman was suffocated on 11th August, 1884 when the shaft collapsed, stopping ventilation.

Whittle

Located 4.5 miles south of Alnwick on the east side of the Great North Road – now the A1, near Newton on the Moor, Whittle had been a source of coal for generations. It is known that prior to 1576 burgesses from Alnwick were extracting coal from small pits at that location; and in 1685 Whittle Colliery was owned by Thomas Gilbert, Gilbert Swinhoe and later Timothy Davison and Matthew Jefferson.

In 1913 an Indenture gave Ellen Garwood of London, Mr H.A Paynter and Mr N. Dunn permission to open a drift mine at Whittle and to develop a tramway system to carry away the product of the mine.

Originally Whittle was owned by South Shilbottle Collieries (later South Shilbottle Collieries (1928) Limited. Like Shilbottle Grange Pit it was bought by the Co-operative Wholesale Society in January 1928. The manager in 1930 was Mr W.L Varty. In 1947 Whittle was taken over by the National Coal Board, whose name changed to British Coal in 1986.

In 1938 the CWS agreed to drive a more sophisticated drift at Whittle and sink a new pit to serve Shilbottle Colliery. The outbreak of the Second World War halted those developments. However, in 1946 the new drift at Whittle was started and reached coal in 1947 when a second drift was driven at a steep gradient for a return airway. Between 1961 and 1965 the National Coal Board further developed Whittle by driving a new surface drift, ultimately increasing the combined daily output of Shilbottle and Whittle to 2500 tons.

The entrance to Whittle Colliery is concealed in a dip situated south of the link road to the settlement of Hampeth off the east exit of the A1 road. Except for miners and tradesmen visiting the drift mine, few people will have seen the extent of the surface buildings, which the images on page 37 aptly reveal.

Whittle Colliery worked the Shilbottle Seam and initially produced around 55,000 tons of household coal per year. In 1921 it employed 117 men; 73 of them worked underground.

A diesel/electric train (class 0-8) shunting empty tubs towards the screens and workshops at Whittle.

Ken Middlemist collection

The screens and workshops at Whittle. A mineral line, to deliver coal from Whittle to a siding near the NER main line near South Side south of Warkworth Station was laid shortly after the CWS took ownership of Whittle Colliery.

Ken Middlemist collection

The railway line shown in the map was driven five miles south and then east past Hazon, Bank House, Brotherwick, under the roadway to South Side interchange sidings, before connecting to the East Coast Main Line. Initially there were three sidings at South Side and later six.

reproduced with permission of Northumberland Records Office

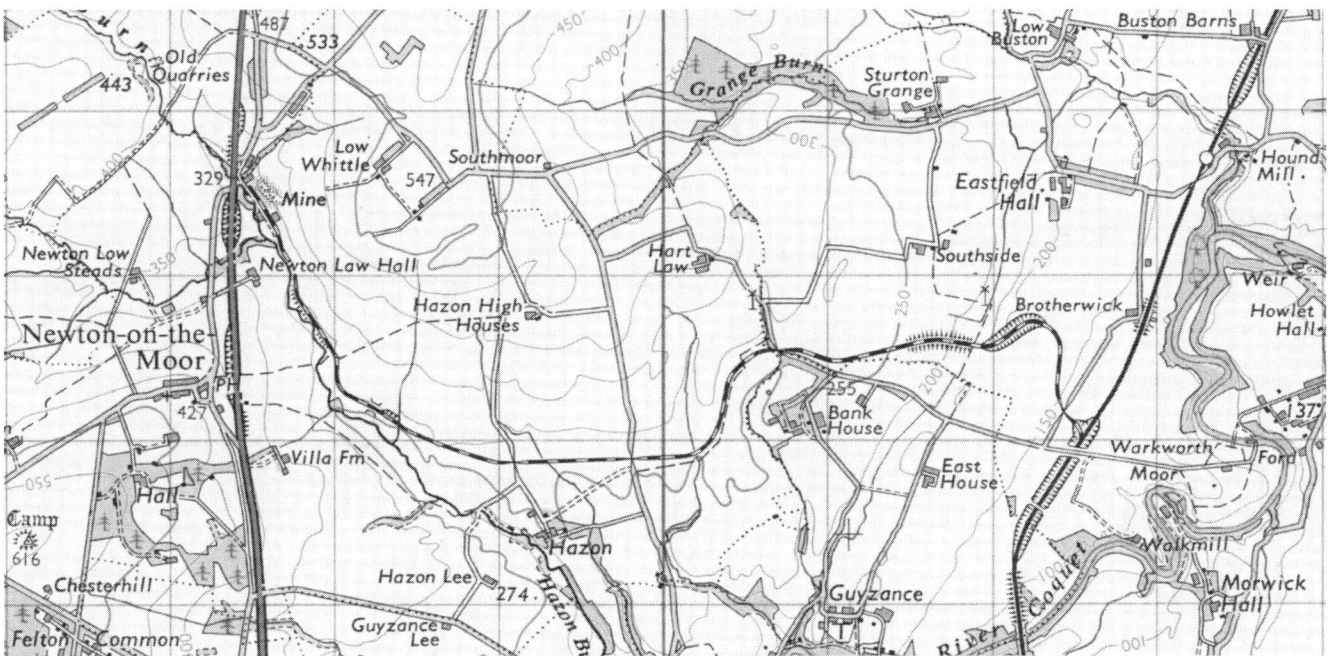

Left: Trains (Giesl-fitted 'Austerity' 0-6-0ST numbers 31 and 33) leaving Whittle colliery.

Centre: Making way to the exchange sidings at South-Side towards the East Coast Main Line.

Bottom: At approximately the same location, showing an original 'Austerity' steam locomotive and its subsequent replacement.
All Ken Middlemist collection

Whittle Colliery yard in 1972. *Tom Heavyside*

The new drift developed by the NCB was situated approximately 1.5 miles from the old one. It was 500 metres long, dipping at a gradient of one in three. This drift was producing coal by 1966 and at its peak it produced 700,000 tons of coal per year. Initially, Whittle was belt fed all the way to the drift entrance, where the coal was loaded into wagons and taken back to the screens on a standard gauge track. There was also a narrow gauge track for conveying men from the pithead baths to the drift and for transporting materials. Initially the colliery worked the same methods as Shilbottle with 60, 80 and 100 yard hand-filling faces. Later, under the NCB, 120 yard faces were 'bottom cut', fired by explosives then hand-filled.

Longframlington Colliery's connection with Whittle

Longframlington Colliery was also owned by Shilbottle Collieries Limited and was located three miles west of Whittle. A ropeway connecting the two delivered 32 tubs per hour to Whittle, over pylons 35 feet high and was powered by a six-horsepower engine.

In 1970 there were 626 workmen employed at Whittle, 515 underground; and at its peak, in 1975, it employed 648 men, 537 underground. Two years before it closed Whittle had 205 men working underground and 206 on the surface.

Adrian Brent coming off the particularly wet Y103 face at Whittle. *Davy Dunn collection*

This 1905 photograph of Longframlington was taken prior to the construction of the aerial ropeway to Whittle *John Ryan collection*

Aerial ropeway from Longframlington to Whittle.
Ken Middlemist collection

Longframlington electric narrow gauge railway.
Ken Middlemist collection

By this stage it had a narrow gauge electric engine working underground on its single gauge 'Main Roadway.'

Because of difficulties in accessing coal west of the shaft towards the Whin Fault, which separated underground workings between Whittle and Shilbottle Collieries, the management at Shilbottle began to consider the feasibility of combining Shilbottle with Whittle by forging a connecting road from Whittle so that thereafter Whittle could be used as the main extraction point and entrance for workers, equipment and supplies. Preliminary discussion began in 1975 and more detailed meetings took place between 1976 and December 1977.

Thyssen's Mining Contractors GB were contracted to complete the tunnelling work which started on 22nd November 1976. Inevitably there were delays arising from NUM workers at the colliery having issues with Thyssen's men accessing their equipment and carrying out work which could have been completed by colliers. Once these issues and stoppages were resolved, work-study engineers, Thyssen's staff and colliery officials met weekly as the work progressed. The plan was to forge a link road from Whittle's '10 West' face to connect with Shilbottle's 'Y17 face'. The proposal was to tunnel a twenty yard 'drivage' through the solid workings. A 'bunker' was to be created on the Shilbottle side alongside the Y17 face-line, with the remodelling of the Y17 tailgate with arches modified from 10 feet to 14 feet, with dual tracking sufficient for 6 man-riding cars (108 men), these cars to be used for supply delivery underground once the men had been despatched. A 200 HP, 36 inch conveyor was part of the proposal. Once the underground work was completed the surface configuration was to be modified to accommodate men, materials and extracted coal.

The key personnel involved in the planning were Shilbottle's under manager Mr W.T Wayman, who chaired the meetings; Mr C. Miller – manager at Whittle; and the electrical, mechanical and planning engineers i.e. J. Forster, E. Stanbury and J.S. Scott, the latter three men from Shilbottle.

The planning team met finally on 19th December 1977 and the Shilbottle/Whittle 'Combination' was completed by the end of that year.

In August 1976, the capital costs of creating the connection was predicted to be £54,216 and the estimated cost for creating a 'drivage' of 100 yards, including revenue costs, was £75,000. The total cost for the 'Combination' is not recorded in the papers,* but inevitably stoppages, delays in delivering materials and technical difficulties would escalate the costs.

On 4th October 1982 Shilbottle ceased production and the workers transferred to Whittle Drift, where they continued to work the same coal faces they had worked from Shilbottle.

In 1982 it was decided to install 240 yard shearer faces at Whittle Colliery. Soon afterwards it was found that the smallest available 34 inch coal shearing machines could not operate successfully in a 28 inch seam. Hand-working the face, as had been the case for years, could have continued.

The North Shaft in the process of being professionally capped in 1982.

Dave Young collection

Shilbottle Colliery after closure.

Graham Knox collection

---

*   Mr W.T. Wayman's Plans and papers 'Specifications of Underground Workings at Shilbottle Colliery' and 'NCB Method Study papers report B243/W/8' referring to Whittle/Shilbottle Combination dated 1976/77.

Photographs of Shilbottle Colliery after closure with the surface buildings being cleared in 1981, 'awaiting the scrapman' after the mine entrance at Shilbottle had closed.
Graham Knox collection

National Mineworkers' Strikes

In the 1960s mineworkers were paid significantly more than workers in other industries but over twelve or more years, despite the men working long unsocial hours in dangerous conditions, their take home pay had slipped below other industrial workers. In the West Yorkshire coalfield older, less able surface workers were required to work longer hours for less money than 'coal winning' underground miners and when the miners' appeal for salary increases was rejected the workforce went on unofficial strike. Arthur Scargill rose to prominence during this strike which drew in collieries as far afield as Scotland. The pay and conditions claim of the West Yorkshire miners was settled in three weeks and the miners returned to work.

The 1969 strike was a significant turning point in industrial relations and spawned other strike action by miners, and in 1972 Shilbottle colliery's workforce went on strike as part of an officially sanctioned strike for action for better pay by the National Union of Mineworkers. During this short strike, tension between families, aggressive picketing and long lasting animosities arose because the National Association of Colliery Overmen and Deputies, and the Shot Firers' Union did not join the strike. An unprecedented cold spell and significant voltage cuts in power resulting in the timed closure of parts of the National Grid system ended the strike after seven weeks with an improved pay offer. The men returned to work on 28th February 1972.

Tensions across the village did not end. Financial hardship, the reduction of essential creature comforts such as food and warmth, bordering in some families on poverty and extreme deprivation, had a long lasting impact with tensions between workmen who continued to work, and therefore earn, being compared with those whose families experienced lasting hardship. The tensions endured, and in some cases, still exist.

The official N.U.M. national mineworkers strike between 6th March 1984 and 3rd March 1985 certainly led to the closure, by Margaret Thatcher's Conservative Government, of many collieries across the country and it may have been an additional factor in British Coal's decision to close Whittle Colliery on 27th March 1987.

For a period, Whittle was privately owned by E.R.S. Mining Development (NE) Ltd and then Whittle Colliery Ltd. Both companies continued to produce coal for the household market.

The Management of Shilbottle Colliery

Between 1921 and 1940, the colliery was manged by Mr Coverdale S. Anderson. His under-manager was Mr J. Scott.

Mr Stan Robson took over as manager in 1960 and his deputies until 1965 were Herbert Swinburn, Mr J. Lawson and then Mr W. Terry Wayman.

In 1945 Mr J.G. Charlton became manager his under-manager being Mr E.K. Anderson, until 1950 when Mr J. Stoker was appointed to that position. The men pictured on the upper row left to right: Manager J.G. Charleton and Head Engineer William Dixon. Lower row left to right: Foreoverman Harry Air, agent for the NCB area W. Gibson and another photograph of J.G. Charleton.

John Stewart collection

Fatalities At Shilbottle Colliery

The Durham Mining Museum lists the following incomplete details of men who were killed at the Grange Pit, or died following injuries underground at the colliery, between 1926 and 1973.

NAME	AGE	DATE	CAUSE
Henry Wilson,	52	5.6.1937	Septic infection*
William Cunningham		28.6.1934	Accident
Henry Stewart	38	8.11.1934	Fall of Stone
Norman Peebles	33	22.8.1938	Accident
Robert Septimus Shell	33	1.3.1938	Fall of stone
Joseph Connell	28	24.6.1939	Fall of stone
William (Kit) Alder	46	14.5.1940	Explosion
John Wilson	52	16.5.1940	Explosion
William Nicholson	48	22.5.1940	Explosion
Stephen Boyd	35	8.9.1941	Fall of stone
Frederick J. Miller	35	31.10.1941	Fall of stone
John Wilkinson	28	1.2.1951	Fall of stone
Henry Donaldson	52	9.5.1951	Fall of stone
David Hewitt	35	7.5.1953	Fall of stone
Charles Purshaw		25.6.1953	Collapsed
Ralph Gray	27	27.5.1957	Fall of stone
John Robert Scott	36	12.4.1958	Crushed
Kenneth Queen	40	May 1960	Accident
Frederick William Young	50	19.7.1968	Accident
Andrew Boyd	57	Feb. 1973	Accident
Robert H. York	40	May 1973	Accident

The Durham Mining Museum's records provide the following enhanced information about these fatalities.

Henry WILSON, aged 41, of 2 Monkhouse Terrace, Alnwick was seriously injured by a fall of stone in Shilbottle Colliery on 25th January 1926, as a consequence of this he was totally paralysed. Eleven years later, on 5th June, 1937 he died of septic infection, aged 52.

William CUNNINGHAM, a putter, born at Radcliffe, was injured and died in Shilbottle Colliery on 28th June, 1934.

Mr Cunningham had signed for Liverpool Football Club in 1920. He played three times for the first team, at left half. His other clubs were Blyth Spartans, Barrow and Mid Rhondda.

Henry STEWART, 38 years of age, of Shilbottle Grange was killed by a fall of stone on 8th November 1934. He was married with three sons.

His funeral took place on 11th November (Armistice Day). The *Northumberland Gazette* reported that 'Mr Stewart had a fine record of war service, rising from the rank of Sergeant in the Alnwick company of the 7th Battalion of the Northumberland Fusiliers. He went to France with the 50th division and took part in the battle of Ypres – he was later granted a commission and rose to the rank of Lieutenant ... Shilbottle and Alnwick branches of the British Legion ... marched to the church where they formed a double guard of honour through which his coffin was borne. The last rites were conducted by the Rev W Robson of the parish. The members of the Legion formed a circle round the grave and after 2 minutes silence they filed past, each in turn dropping a Flanders Poppy on to the coffin.

Norman PEEBLES, aged 33 years, of Shilbottle died following an accident at the colliery on 22nd August, 1938.

Robert Septimus SHELL, aged 33 of 17 Percy Road, Shilbottle, a coal filler died in the colliery on 1st March 1938, following the fall of stone measuring 9ft, by 3ft 9 inches by 14 inches. The Coroner's jury carefully considered the safety and placing of props, examined the deputy Henry Ogle about his inspection of the workplace and heard evidence from Mr Shell's colleague Thomas Swordy. The jury returned a verdict of accidental death.

Joseph CONNELL, 28 years of 2, Eastgarth Avenue, Amble was killed on 24th June, 1939 when stone fell on him while using a coal cutting machine underground. The inquest, held in Amble Courthouse by Coroner Mr H. J. Percy in the presence of the Colliery Manager C.S. Anderson, Mr T. A. Rogers, Mines Inspector, Police Superintendent Spratt and Mr G. Bartram representing the Northumberland Miners' Association, considered the sufficiency and placing of the timbers propping up the roof prior to cutting. After hearing the evidence, the jury returned a verdict of accidental death.

Mr Connell left a widow and child. His brother John Connell, aged 15 was killed at Broomhill Colliery on 24th February, 1924.

William (Kit) ALDER coal filler aged 46 of Church Lane, Warkworth, was one of eight miners who on 14th May 1940 were seriously burnt and injured as a result of an explosion due to the ignition of fire damp in the colliery. Mr Alder died at Alnwick Infirmary on 16th May 1940. The cause of death was shock as a result of burns arising from an explosion of gas.

The injured were taken to Alnwick Infirmary, and were seen at once by a doctor who administered first aid. Two other miners died.

An inquest, enlarged to cover the purposes of a Governmental inquiry, was held over three days – 24th – 26th July 1940 at Alnwick Courthouse. During the inquest 'the quality of the powder used for firing the shots and ventilation were brought into question. The particular (black) powder was not supposed to be used, but Shilbottle Colliery had applied for an exemption in 1937. An accumulation of gas had occurred whilst the filler was drilling out and the firing of the shot ignited a flame which travelled approximately sixty yards down the face. Coked dust, singed props, burned papers and a roar of flames was heard.

Some of the miners who were amongst those injured by the explosion described how, following the report of the explosion a sheet of flame swept past and the roar of the flames was heard.

At the end of the inquiry, the Coroner recommended that the existing law should be amended so that where any inflammable gas was discovered in a coal mine, that it should be reported to the Inspector of Mines, and the Inspector should be empowered, in his discretion, to order that first of all safety lamps must be used, and second, that permitted explosives only should be used, until he permitted to the contrary.

John WILSON, Deputy, aged 52 died 17th May leaving a widow and two children.

The burial of Mr Wilson was reported in the Morpeth Herald on 24th May.

The funeral of Mr John Wilson ... took place at Shilbottle on Monday (20th May 1940) when there was a very large attendance of mourners, including colliery officials, many workmen, Freemasons, and representatives of all the institutions of the village. The vicar, the Rev H. G. Cutter, conducted the service and the interment at the churchyard.

---

* Henry Wilson was injured and paralysed on 25th June 1926. He died 11 years later.

Mr C.S. Anderson (manager) Mr J. G. Charlton (under manager) of Shilbottle Colliery, Mr T. Dobson Under manager of Whittle Colliery at Hampeth, represented officials of the Co-operative Society, and Mr C. H. Brookbanks (Chairman) of the Deputies' Association.'

William NICHOLSON coal filler, aged 48 of 8 Colliers Close, Shilbottle – injured in the explosion died on 22nd May. His death was widely reported, including the *Gloucester Citizen* newspaper for 23rd May 1940. ' ... the third victim of last week's explosion in the Co-operative Wholesale Society's colliery at Shilbottle, Northumberland, died in Alnwick Infirmary. He leaves a widow (Elizabeth Lillian) and 11 children.' Two of Mr Nicholson's sons also worked at the pit. There were six little ones.

Also injured were **W. BASTON, Alex MITCHISON, J. PENDLETON, Mark SWAN, J. WEIGHTMAN.**

Others who formed the rescue party were the engineer Mr W. Dixon, Mr W. Little (Overman) and the Manager Mr J. G. Charlton.

Stephen BOYD, colliery deputy, aged 54 years of South East Farm, Shilbottle was killed on 8th September, 1941 when he was hit by a tub which had jumped the points, having according to the Coroner Mr H.J. Percy, failed to observe all precautions for safety.

Frederick J MILLER, aged 35 of Church Street, Amble was killed by a fall of stone on 31st October 1941.

At the inquest into his death on 7th November 1941, practical suggestions were made before the Coroner Mr Hugh J Percy by Mr F W Bertram (The Miners' Association) for improving the timbering of the roof in certain conditions. These suggestions were accepted by one of the colliery Deputies Mr J Stuart. The manager, Mr Coverdale S Anderson said, 'We will take every precaution for the better protection of our men.

John WILKINSON, aged 28 of 2 Percy Road, Shilbottle suffered a fractured pelvis and other injuries following a fall of a 4ft long, 3ft wide and 2ft 9in thick piece of stone which fell, owing to a flaw in it, on 1st February 1951. He was moved to Alnwick Infirmary and then Ashington Hospital later that day, where he died. The inquest into his death examined safety issues before pronouncing a verdict of 'Death by Misadventure'.

Henry DONALDSON, coal filler aged 52 years, of 3 Colliers' Close, Shilbottle, was killed by a fall of stone on 9th May 1951. He left a widow and adult daughter.

David HEWITT, aged 35 of 43 St. Thomas' Crescent, Alnwick died of haemorrhage following a fall of stone on 7th May 1953.

Charles PURSHAW, of 8 King Street, Alnwick collapsed and died underground on 25th June 1953. He was identified by his son Charles Purshaw of 3 Dukes Memorial Cottages, Alnwick.

Ralph GRAY, aged 27 years, of Howling Lane, Alnwick was killed by a stone 5ft long, 2ft wide and 10 inches thick crashing into him on 27th May 1957.

John Robert SCOTT, 36 years was crushed by a cutting machine 2nd April 1958. He died from his injuries 10 days later in Ashington Hospital on 12th April 1958.

Kenneth QUEEN, aged 40 died as a result of injuries sustained at Shilbottle Colliery in May 1960.

Frederick William YOUNG, aged 50 died, following an accident on 19th July 1968. He left his wife Dorothy and a son Foster Young.

Andrew BOYD, 57 years, an overman, formerly of Radcliffe and Hauxley Colliery, was killed underground at Shilbottle Colliery in February 1973.

Robert H. YORK, 40 years of age, was killed underground at Shilbottle Colliery in May 1973.

Fatalities At Whittle Colliery

The Amble and District Mining Memorial records seven fatalities at Whittle Colliery as follows:

NAME	AGE	DATE	CAUSE
William Athey CAMPBELL	16	22.11.1937	Killed by a runaway tub
William NEAL	27	20.5.1938	Crushed by a fall of stone
James HUTCHINSON	33	18.11.1938	Crushed by an empty tub
Richard (Dickie) DENT	37	18.10.1946	Crushed by a fall of stone
George GRAHAM	49	13.2.1948	Suffocated after falling into a wagon containing loose coal
James HENDERSON		1965**	
Ian Arthur HEGGARTY	28	1986.	

Pit pony in Shilbottle Colliery.

---

*   Fourteen other deaths in the 18th, 19th and 20th century, not previously recorded in local history publications, are known to have occurred in Shilbottle collieries. These are shown at Appendix 1.

**   The exact date of the last two fatalities, the age of Mr Henderson and circumstances of both fatalities have regrettably not been determined, and for this the author apologises to the deceased's relatives.

Following the closure of the collieries the spoil heap east of the colliery at Shilbottle Grange was landscaped and planted with grass and coniferous trees. The photograph shows the heap in 1988 after it had been landscaped and planted. Initially the planting was done by hand but later a tractor with two men could plant 600 to 1,000 young trees per day. The trees took three years to become properly established.

Courtesy of David Baillie, Forestry Officer, Northumberland County Council 1973-2007

The stone building, formerly the manager's office and caretaker/baths superintendent's house, is the only remaining building on the former colliery site. It is now a private dwelling. Any visitor to Shilbottle, unfamiliar with its history would not be able to discern that a coal mine had once been entered at this location. Indeed, within the village, there is little to reflect its industrial past. The end of mining in Shilbottle parish marked the end of an era, affected the economic security of most residents in the village and altered the very fabric of the community.

Author's collection

Appendix 1

Deaths in Shilbottle Collieries, or attributed to working at one of the Shilbottle Collieries in the 18th, 19th and 20th centuries, and whilst shown on the Shilbottle memorial are not previously recorded in local history publications.

February/March 1775	Brown, Thomas – choked on foul air.
24.12.1815	Brown, David 52 years – choked on foul air. Dobson, John 74 years – choked on foul air. Jeffrey, Thomas, 44 years – choked on foul air. Jeffrey, John, 16 years – choked on foul air.
23.1.1856	Snaith, Robert – fall of stone.
31.4.1858	Henderson, Joseph, 15 years – fall from descent chain.
4.5.1860	Weightman, John, 48 years, depression, possible suicide following Emphysema caused by dust inhalation.
16.1.1863	Ogle, Thomas, 30 years, fall of stone.
4.11.1876	Young, Matthew, 17 years, found dead in disused coal pit, after drinking alcohol.
December 1914	Baxter, Charles, 54 years, crushed in garden by passing coal tub.
22.4.1920	Hannah, Albert Edward, 20 years, heart attack following crush injuries underground.

Shilbottle Colliery's No. 51, a class '10' diesel, formerly British Rail's D4056, built in 1961, it worked for 11 years in Yorkshire and Lincolnshire before it was withdrawn in June 1972. It was acquired by the NCB and served the remainder of its working life at Shilbottle until it was broken up, in March 1983, following the closure of the colliery. *Courtesy Roy Lambeth Durham Mining Museum*

Religion in Shilbottle

The worship of Jesus Christ in Shilbottle has a history which can be traced to at least the 13th century. It is thought that a wooden or stone place of worship was built on the present site of St. James' Church, probably by the Tisons, before the stone church of St. James' was built and then remodelled in 1884.

The Norman church consisted of a nave 56 feet in length and 25 feet wide, with a chancel of 32 feet by 22 feet. It had a porch and vestry and slit windows, before they were enlarged and fitted with window sashes.

In the 13th century the church of Shilbottle was acquired by the abbot and convent of Alnwick and in 1292 records of taxation within the archdeaconry of Northumberland show that the rectory of 'Shilbotill' was assessed at £12 2 shillings towards the expense of the Crusades.

Shilbottle continued to be served by a secular priest until the middle of the 14th century when, on 31st July 1331, Lewis Beaumont, Bishop of Durham granted a licence to allow that *henceforth the canons might present one of themselves to the benefice.* From this time onward, to the dissolution of religious houses, the history of the benefice is merged with that of Alnwick Abbey. After the Reformation the 'advowson'* remained in the Crown until 1892 when it was transferred to the Duke of Northumberland.

The roof of St. James' Church in 1715 was flat and covered in lead before being raised and slated, probably in 1790. The western gable had a belfry with two bells. The south doorway had a circular arch which was retained when the church was later remodelled. The chancel arch, of two square orders with chamfered label and impost, was later adapted as the arch of the north transept. Over the entrance of the porch is a Latin inscription

SHILBOTTLE CHURCH IN 1824.

Joseph Cook's drawing showing the church in 1824.

Shilbottle Church in the 19th century prior to alteration. *Jean Hall collection*

Shilbottle Church following the alterations which were completed in 1884. *Author's collection*

---

* An 'advowson' was the right to recommend a member of the Anglican clergy for a vacant benefice or to make an appointment.

dated MDCCCXVIII (1818) which names two incumbents: Johannes Salkeld and Josephus Cook.

The first chaplain recorded for the parish of Shilbottle (Siplibotle) was Richard in 1228. Throughout the decades a further 31 chaplains or vicars are recorded up to 1880 when Joseph Golightly was installed. (see *www.fusilier/co/uk/shilbottle/st_james_church*)

The Duke of Northumberland's Business Minutes, Vol II for the period April to September 1848 refer to representations made by the vicar of Shilbottle, the Rev. W.Y Smythies, proposing material improvements to St. James' Church and seeking financial support from the Duke for work estimated to be worth £91 10s. The application was subsequently debated, taking into account existing rental of glebe lands, resulting in the approval of the sum of £36 12s. as a contribution towards the cost of the alterations.

The modifications were carried out under the supervision of architect W.S. Hicks over an extended period. The church, *which had been damaged by wind and weather and the interior ravaged by woodworm*, was re-consecrated for worship soon after the creation of Newcastle Diocese, on 18th October 1885, by Bishop Ernest Wilberforce, grandson of the famous slave trade abolitionist.

According to the *Alnwick Mercury* 14th October 1885 the preacher was the Reverend J.J. Perry; prayers were 'intoned by the Rev J. Golightly.'

The 'new' church was described by Nikolaus Pevsner in *The buildings of England: Northumberland* as being 'impressive, cruciform (in design) with a strong crossing tower and taller octagonal stair turret ... the former chancel arch (now serving as the organ chamber).'

By 1885 the churchyard, consisting of 1100 square yards, had sufficient space for three or four more graves. The church's submission to extend the burial ground by a further 1333 square yards was approved. In August 1911 a further similar size extension of the burial ground, expected to serve the church and the village for 30 years, was agreed.

Extracts from the Shilbottle registers for baptisms, weddings and funerals.

1697,   May 30th Roger, son of Cuthbert Buston of Woodhouse was baptised.

1698/9   Jan 26th Eleanor, wife of Daniel Selby of Shilbottle was buried.

1713   July 9th Mark Ogle of Pont Island (Ponteland) parish and Mrs Elizabeth Manners of Acton, Felton parish were married.

1733   Sept 15th Thomas Wardle of the parish of Framlington and Mary Strother of this parish – married.

1766   May 23rd John Laing and Sarah Nicholson, both of Hazon, married

1802   Oct 28th Maria Alicia, third daughter of George William Leeds, of Low Newton Esq., a native of St. Margaret, Westminster, by his wife Maria Sanderson, a native of Morpeth, baptised.

F.R. Wilson's drawing of St. James Church and Pele Tower and ground plan of the church before the rebuilding of the church in 1884.

Some miscellaneous matters:

1577-1587   The vicarage at Shilbotle was valued at £4 14s. 8d.
1663   The vicar's stipend was £20 p.a.
1665   The parish contributed 4s. 9d. to the relief of sufferers from the great plague of London.
1826   The vicarage at Shilbottle was valued at £220.
1868   Mr Hugh Taylor of Earsdon, commissioner to the Duke of Northumberland, in his will gave £1,000 to the vicar of Shilbottle, the interest on which was to be distributed to the poor each Christmas.

Joseph Cook was vicar between 1803 and 1844. He combined his positions of squire and parson, living at Newton Hall. In 1835 when he celebrated the golden jubilee of his ordination members of the congregation presented him with a set of silver communion vessels and a baptismal bowl, which he donated to the church as a thanksgiving.

The first couple to be married in the remodelled church were Sir Edward Grey (Foreign Secretary between 1905-1916, later Viscount Grey of Fallodon) and Miss Dorothy Widdrington of Newton Hall on 20th October, 1885.

Dorothy died on 4th February, 1906 in a road accident.

Recent clergy-incumbents of the Parish of Shilbottle

1900 – 1921   Percy Thomas Lee.
1921 – 1935   William Robson.
1935 – 1936   John Simpson Turnbull.
1936 – 1945   Harry Gordon Cutter.
1945 – 1956   William Hume.
1956 – 1959   Henry Ball.
1959 – 1966   Alfred Edward Collinson.
1966 – 1976   Terence Maud Oliver.
1976 – 1982   Hedley Scott.
1983 – 1988   Peter Lister.
1989 – 1996   Richard Glover.
1998 – 2008   Edward Michael Dixon.
2009 – 2011   Anthony Cavanagh.
2013 – 2017   Martin Gillham.
2019 –   Helen O'Sullivan.

The Memories of Shilbottle states that Reverend Percy Thomas Lee 'was chairman of the Parish Council at the beginning of the 20th century. He played an important and vital role in the life of the village. Villagers were so appreciative of his efforts that they named Lee Avenue in his memory'.

St. James' Church Choir during Reverend Lee's incumbency.

A confirmation group at St. James Church in the 1950, Reverend Hume is in the background, in the group are Carol Inglis and Irene Brand.

Carol Hope (née Inglis) collection

Reverend Michael Dixon was also one of the chaplains at H.M. Prison at Acklington. He was succeeded by Reverend Martin John Gillham as a house for duty priest. Mrs Patricia Eleanor Rennison, a former Reader at Shilbottle, was ordained as a Local Minister 2011. She retired in 2018 as did Martin Gillham. During a long interregnum services were conducted by retired priests living in the village or from elsewhere in the diocese.

Reverend Helen O'Sullivan was licensed to the parish in 2019; her responsibilities were extended by the Privy Council to cover Warkworth and Acklington as part of a new benefice.

Some Features of St. James' Church

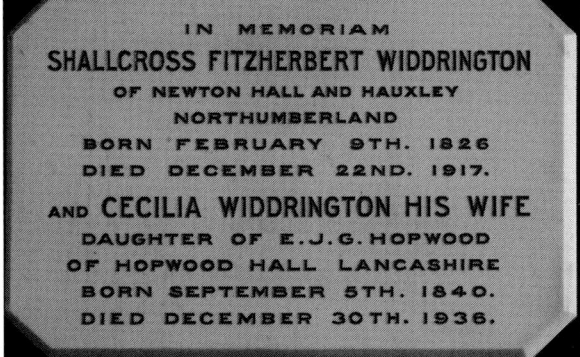

Above: Commemorative plaque for Shallcroft Fitzherbert Widdrington who was Lord of Newton Hall and Manor, chief land owner, Justice of the Peace and High Sheriff of Northumberland in 1874; and his wife Cecilia.

Left: The original Norman font, from the old church stands close to the entrance door. It has had carved decorations added to the bowl in more recent times. *Right*: The decorative font ewer dated 1899.

Shilbottle' Church Hut

In 1921 St. James' Church paid for and had erected a hut in Shilbotle Grange. The intention was for it to be used for worship and community activies in the east end of the village. It was still being used in 1954 for weddings, Women's Institute meetings and other social events.

Shilbottle's Medieval Defensive Pele Tower

The tower* is believed to have originally been owned by Henry Percy, the first Earl of Northumberland in 1367. It was later forfeited to the Crown and passed by Henry IV to his son John, Duke of Bedford. It was under his ownership that the Pele Tower appears in the 1415 list of castles and fortalices in the Harleian manuscripts, which were compiled for King Henry V to inform him of his strength on the Scottish Border before he left for his battle in Agincourt.

Subsequently, Shilbottle was held by Alexander de Hilton before being passed to Robert de Hilton during the early to mid 14th century. The tower did not revert back to Northumberland on their restoration in 1416 but was inherited in 1435 by Henry VI, then granted to Robert Lord Ogle. The Percy family had reacquired the property by 1472.

The house has changed externally and internally several times. It has been speculated that because of the smallness of the tower, there may have once been a second larger one.

At the time of the renovations the stone mason has inscribed at the foot of the tower, words believed to have been copied from a tomb in Melrose Abbey:

> Earth builds on earth, castles and towers. To earth, saith the earth, all shall be ours.

Reverend J.B. Roberts was vicar between 1849 and 1880. His wife Sophia is buried in the churchyard. Her tombstone has a beautiful inscription.

> Beneath this column, in the shade of the Yews, planted by her own hand, reposes the mortal frame in form and aspect fair, of Sophia Roberts, the faithful, loving and beloved wife of John B. Roberts M.A. E.L.M. Cantab., Vicar of Shilbottle. This gentle woman "in whose spirit was no guile" so tender as a parent: amiable as an acquaintance, warm-hearted as a friend of humanity: peacefully fell asleep in the arms of the Christian graces, faith, hope charity: who bore her better half away to the spirit land. Feby 7th 1867. "Sleep to waken in a brighter world."

The ages of her living children – 12, 20, 26, 27 and 28 are recorded. She bore twelve children but the details have worn away.

The east side of the Pele Tower with vicarage attached.

---

* Information about the Pele Tower and vicarage has been extracted from research papers prepared by Mrs Pam Vardy who lived with her husband in the Pele House from 1986 – 2020.

The front of the Pele Tower/House from the road leading north past the church.

The east facing Pele Tower and former Tythe Barn was converted in 1863 into a dining room with a drawing room above for Reverend J.B. Roberts.

Methodism in Shilbottle Parish

For 140 years the Jubilee Hall at Newton on the Moor was used for worship and a Methodist chapel stood at the west end of the village close to Newton on the Moor's school. The 'New Connexion' chapel was on land given by Captain Widdrington and was used for 100 years from 1842 as a place of worship. There was also a Methodist chapel next to Percy House at the west end of North Side in Shilbottle.

On 15th January 1924, following representations made on behalf the people of Shilbottle and Bilton Banks* by the Reverend Frederick Leonard Hines of Wesley House, Amble to the executive directors of the Co-operative Wholesale Society in Manchester, Hines was given approval to possess and build a Methodist Connexion chapel, as a place of religious worship, on a quarter acre site at the north end of Hawthorn Terrace in Shilbottle.

The visiting superintendent minister was the Reverend Hines from Amble, but local lay preachers included Mr Bartram who cycled from Felton, and two local men, Mr Arnold Chrisp, who was also one of Shilbottle Colliery's overmen, and Mr Lowdy Lang. The chapel was exceptionally well attended, especially by young people from the colliery houses at the east end of the village who were issued each week with gummed stamps depicting Saints and notable Christian missionaries. The Chapel closed as a place of worship in 1977.

After standing unattended for a period, the chapel was sold to a tradesman who restored washing machines and other electrical appliances before being demolished in the 1990s. On the site there now stand two large detached houses.

Shilbottle's Gateway Church

There is a Gateway Church** in Shilbottle which meets in the Community Hall.***

Shilbottle Methodist Chapel. *Kenneth Wilcox collection*

---

*   There were fourteen signatures attached to the petition, including Edward Anderson, Edward Kinghorn, John Varty, Anthony Dunbar and Reverend Frederick Leonard Hines.
** The Gateway Church is a Bible-based, evangelical, Spirit-empowered church founded in 2000 by Pastor Robert Morris in America.
*** Numerous other activities take place in the Community Hall, including two youth groups, the W.I., and a Badminton Club

Education in Shilbottle

The Church of England School, Shilbottle c. 1900.

Church sponsored education in Northumberland began with King Oswald inviting the abbot of Iona to send someone to evangelise his kingdom, followed by St. Aidan arriving on Lindisfarne in AD 635 to open a school of learning for the next generation of monks. To Aidan's school came twelve boys who were to prove to be St. Aidan's successors, among them Chad, Cedd and Wilfred through whom the gospel was spread as they founded religious communities across Yorkshire, the Midlands and Essex. So the Church in Northumberland grew with the understanding that care and education for the next generation was a priority. Throughout the later medieval period most monastic foundations included educational opportunities for the sons and sometimes daughters of local people. We know that Shilbottle's church of St. James was associated with Alnwick Abbey, and whilst there is no evidence of lay education taking place in Hulne Park, it seems reasonable to assume there was some.

In 1648, at the start of the Commonwealth, the vicar was 'turned out' but restored in 1660. During this time he was *forbid to keep school or to use the Common Prayer in a private congregation in his own house.* The implication here is that he had previously offered basic education to boys. In 1663 it is recorded that in Shilbottle, whilst the church was in good condition, *there were no schools, and neither papists nor sectaries.**

The Henry Strother endowment of £250 in 1751 left in trust portions of the interest of that sum annually to the vicar, the schoolmasters of Shilbottle and Newton on the Moor. It is not clear whether this was to existing schoolmasters or whether the schools were yet to be built. It is, however, certain that in 1866 the Duke's Commissioner, Hugh Taylor, by Deed of Gift, gave the proportion of tithes of Birtley in Chollerton Parish, for education purposes in Shilbottle. The trustees of this gift were the Duke, the Duke's Bailiff and the 'Vicar of Shilbotel'. Of these tithes £20 was paid annually to the master and mistress of Newburn School (where Hugh Taylor's home was located), £2 (less tax and commission of rates) for the maintenance of a 'pant' in the village of Newburn, and the remainder for Shilbottle for the education of twenty poor children. In 1903 this tithe was commuted to £29 4s. 9d. p.a. in trust for Shilbottle School. Hugh Taylor also left £1,000 in 3% consols** for the benefit of the poor of the parish to be distributed by the vicar and church wardens.

We know therefore, that from 1751, for at least a century, the Dukes of Northumberland, who were the principal landowners, provided buildings for a school at the west edge of the village. Later records

---

* *Memories of Shilbottle*, 2000 p 7 from an article published in 1887 by T.F. Bulmer.
** Consols were British government securities without redemption date and with fixed annual interest (i.e. consolidated annuities).

Above: Class of 1882 with Mr John Dunn

Right: A class *c* 1900 The male teacher on the left is thought to be Mr Gerrard. The author's grandfather John Stewart is in the middle of the back row.

Author's collection

Class of 1911 Mr Stone on the left. James Robert Punton is second left from Mr Stone in the back row.

Author's collection

demonstrate that the school closed at lunch time, which meant that children as young as five walked up to four miles, four times a day in all weathers, from outlying farms. It is therefore not surprising that by 1873 attendance could be as low as 50% because of bad weather, illness or the children being required to work in the fields.

In 1870, the school was extended and this allowed the building to accommodate 109 children. By 1922, with the intensification of coal mining and the influx of families, the school catered for 185 children. By the following year, the number had increased to 207. Unable to cope with such an increase, that same year, 25 youngsters left to go to Lesbury School.

Head teachers of the Church School are known to have been:

1851 -1881	Archibald Mitchison.
1881 – 1884	John Dunn.
1884	William Dyson.
1900 – 1913	Mr Mark Gerrard.
1913	Mr J W Stone.
1913 – 1923	Mr John Carr.
1923 – 1930	Mr Hugh Blair Lightfoot.
1930 – 1931	Mr James Sanderson.
1931 – 1951	Mr Andrew Elliot.
1951 – 1979	Mrs Vera McLean.

In 1931 Alice Craggs and C M Bowman acted as head teachers as did Miss Anne Higginson from 1979 to 1981.

In 1852 the school, the property of the Duke of Northumberland, was described, in records held by Northumberland Estates, as

> a cottage with two rooms, with a dairy, wash house, privy and ash pit, the latter in a yard behind the cottage, with a good school room adjoining; all modern erections of stone, covered with blue slate in good state of repair.

The schoolmaster was also postmaster who occupied the cottage. Sixty-five boys and girls attended the school.

Parish records for twenty years later show that following the Education Act of 1870, the school district of Shilbottle and Woodhouse needed a mixed school for 109 children. It was stated that

> If a classroom is at once added ... to accommodate 30 children and a certificated teacher is engaged, no further accommodation will be required.

Class of 1913-14 – headmaster Mr John Carr on the right. James Temple Wilson is in the back row next to the teacher. *Keith Wilson collection*

Class of 1914-15.

In 1874 a new classroom was added, using materials from the nearby condemned Chapel. The 1878 review wanted more, saying, *additional desks are needed but in reality the school should be enlarged*. In 1881 additions were made to the Master's house and in 1887 improvements were made to the school's playground.

The age span of children was 4 -11 when at that age leaving school for work was possible. Most teachers started as pupil teachers on leaving school and were trained on the job. Only a few had the benefit of Teacher Training Colleges and were certificated.

As a Church School, Religious Instruction was inspected separately by the Diocese and a report dated 8th February, 1894 was complimentary:

> This school is again distinctly "excellent" in its Religious Work. The curriculum is varied and comprehensive, and it is seldom that all the Groups of a School so uniformly reach such

a high standard. The children shew keen interest and intelligence, together with a notable enthusiasm in answering. The general average of marks gained in the Prize Scheme was slightly higher than last year. S. Jeffery.

The school log book for 1908 (Northumberland Archives NRO 586, 2359) gives a detailed summary of subject timetables for the older children: the first half hour of every day being for religious instruction and thereafter, throughout the week, in addition, history, elementary science and observation, geography, arithmetic, drill, gardening, needlework, music and for a brief period, shorthand. The infants had their own curriculum and for that there is no specific reference.

The school, by this stage, was providing Elementary education for children up to age 14 from 8.55 am to 4 pm, the school being closed from 12 noon to 1.25 pm. The children were expected to return home at lunchtime to be fed.

School logs show that in 1913, during May and June, the school was disinfected because of an epidemic of diphtheria, and in December of 1916 German measles affected half the school. Until 1916 there are no references to the First World War, despite former pupils and fathers serving and being killed in France. On Monday 11th November, 1918 the school log recorded the signing of the Armistice at 5 am that morning and that hostilities had ceased at 11 am. The news arrived at 2 pm. The children were gathered, the National Anthem was sung and the children dismissed. A holiday was given the following day

In November 1918, the effect of Spanish Flu was beginning to impact and the school was closed by order of the medical officer of health between 22nd November and 9th December and again until 6th January, 1919. It was closed again between 20th March and 7th April, 1920.

Joyce, Jean and Meta Straughan with Andree Elliott, the Church of England's school master's daughter, standing near the wall outside the school circa 1936. The Farrier's Arms public house is in the background. *Susan Armstrong Kirkland collection*

A mixed group of children in the early 1950s outside the Church of England School.

The Parish Room

A choir outside the Parish Room in 1914.
Author's collection

On 4th July, 1923 the children assembled at the west end of Hitchcroft Road to see the Prince of Wales pass by.

For at least 230 years, the Church School provided the only educational opportunities for children in Shilbottle.

With the sinking of the Grange Pit the community virtually doubled in size and to ease the population increase, on 28th April, 1924 the Parish Room became the Infant Teaching Centre.

At the beginning of Mrs McLean's headship in 1951 there were only 32 pupils, this rose to 104 in 1953 but by the time the school closed in 1981 there were only 40. The buildings reverted to the Duke of Northumberland who sold them for residential purposes.

When Shilbottle Grange Colliery was ready to open, and the population of the village increased, the County Council established Shilbottle County School.

Shilbottle's County Primary School

The County Primary School, costing £7,845, is a brick building in Shilbottle Grange built whilst the Grange pit was being sunk in 1925. It remains situated east of the Colliery Welfare Field and above the hill leading to Woodhouse Farm and the colliery. Before it could be brought into use, following officially opening on 26th May, 1926 by County Councillor W.J. Glaholme, of Town Foot, the former mine workings beneath the school had to be excavated to eliminate materials which had started to burn.

The County School was built in the form of a square, with a lawn as the centrepiece. At the time of opening the school had 150 scholars, four classrooms and a large hall, with separate entrances and toilets either side for girls and boys and was centrally heated. Access to the hall was initially through two air-raid shelters, without lights, and the younger children had to be coaxed through these dark tunnels.

The first headmaster was Mr William Davison, who lived in The Crescent, virtually opposite the new school. Standards 1 & 2 shared a room as did Standards 6 & 7. His staff included Miss Thompson who taught infants, Miss Bruce, who also played the piano and Miss Smith who, amongst other subjects, taught knitting and sewing.

At this time the school had an extensive garden for the growing of vegetables.

After Mr Davison's retirement Miss Minnie Dunn, formerly a teacher at Amble Secondary Modern School took over as head teacher.

The north elevation of the school photographed from the nearby Welfare Field – young Gwen Weightman is seen using one of the large swings recently installed there. *Sandra McKnight collection*

Miss Minnie Dunn taught the youngsters to write in italic script and many of them continued to write in that distinctive form throughout their school years and beyond. A few of her students passed their 11 plus grading examination and went to the Duke or Duchess Grammar Schools in Alnwick. The majority went by bus to Amble Secondary Modern School.

Twenty years earlier in 1939, when the country of Northumberland was being prepared for war, the pupils helped tape up the school's windows to minimise the spread of glass in the event of the school buildings being bombed. Drills for air raid precautions were held and Shilbottle was also being prepared to take evacuees.

John Stewart and his wife Margery, living in Kiln Lonnen, were hosts to two evacuees from Carville Road, School in Wallsend on Tyne.

Evacuees inevitably increased the number of students attending the local schools.

During the war attendances occasionally suffered when local farmers asked the head teachers for help in harvesting the potato crop and boys and girls were released for this purpose.

In 1942, drifted snow 3-4 feet deep blocked lanes and roads and disrupted village supplies and school attendance.

Miss Dunn with two of her teachers – Mr Boyd and Mr Holmes.

The Shilbottle County Primary School Choir of 1958 from left to right *Back Row*:
Pamela Gilholm, Pauline Grey, Patricia Munro, Jacqueline Robinson, Miriam Hossain, Kathleen Adamsom. Jennifer Hall, Linda Hudson;
Second Back Row:
Patricia Swordy, Sheila Swinburn, Ian Gibbison, Geofffrey Casson, Raymond Dickie, Carol Casson, Pauline Ternent, Jennifer Tierney;
Second Front Row:
Shuna Bell, Ann Grey, Mary Patton, Jayne Lynn, Anne Nicholson, Sandra Inglis, Jaqueline Grant, Sandra Purvis;
Front Row:
John Punton, Alan Chrisp, John Swinburn, Colin Weightman, Kenneth Robinson, Derek Weightman.

Sandra Stewart (née Purvis) collection

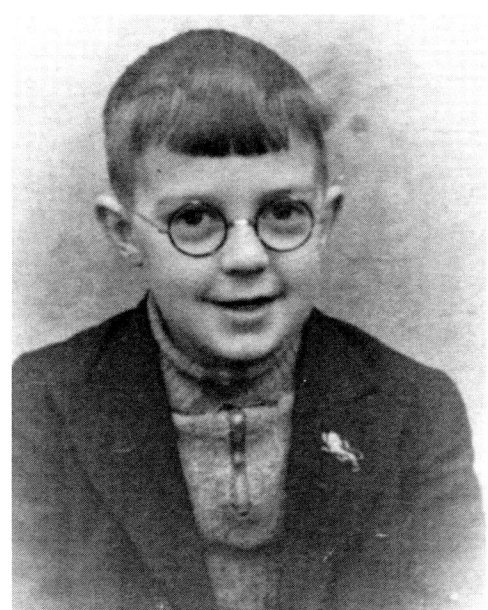

Two of the evacuees: Alan Corbett whilst a resident with the author's grandparents and Lily Rippon, on a return visit after the war.

Members of the cast of the school play in 1958, from left to right.
Brian Watson, Bobby Slater, Jacquie Wilson, Sandra Inglis, Robert Whitehead, Geoffrey Henderson, Jacqueline Grant, Sandra Purvis.
Sandra Stewart (née Purvis) collection

Snowdrifts in the winter of 1942.

Shilbottle's New Housing, Shops, Commercial Outlets and Transport

Housing.

The oldest building, 'Percy Cottage' is on 'West End', the road at the western entrance to the village leading from Denemoor (also known as Hitchcroft) on to North Side.

The indistinct date, above the door-head, is 1707 and with it are the initials F.T.B. In the 18th and early 19th centuries this building was an inn known as the 'Percy Arms.' In 1871 the eldest son of Margaret Muers, the innkeeper at The Farriers Arms public house, married the daughter of the tenant farmer of nearby Colliery Farm. He took over the tenancy of Percy Arms but he continued to work as the blacksmith at the smithy adjacent to the Farriers Arms.

The census data for 1861 to 1891 show Robert Brown as the innkeeper at the Percy Arms as well as being a cartwright and joiner. It is possible that Robert Muers was the licensee, but Robert Brown managed the inn for him.

The Percy Arms played a key role staging the annual village feast over two days. Initially this had taken place at Shilbottle's Black Swan Inn, later the gymnastics, horse and donkey racing of the feast moved to the park of the Percy Arms adjacent to the inn. Throughout the day, the Shilbottle Percy Band played a choice selection of music.

In 1891 the Percy Arms was still trading as an inn, but by the 1940s the property was already known as Percy Cottage. During the following decades Percy Cottage was occupied by Davy and Betsy Henderson. Who ran a taxi service for the village and kept a small holding with byre and pigsties behind the cottage.

Housing

Until the 1920s the village of Shilbottle did not have any long lines of pit houses. The houses were

Percy Cottage (left).

Shilbottle Percy Band performing at the Percy Arms. *Anne Armstrong collection*

David and Betsy Henderson.
Anne Armstrong collection

Percy Road and the Square.
Author's collection

The north end of Percy Road.
Author's collection

North Side looking south.
Author's collection

A view of the Church from Middle Road. *Author's collection*

An early image of Middle Row property, of Keith Wilson's aunt Bessie outside the house where she was born. *Keith Wilson collection*

made of stone in the 18th century and had been built by the Duke of Northumberland's staff and were nearly all situated near St. James' Church. These properties are similar in design to those found in agricultural areas of Northumberland. Originally, there were two short rows of houses, one named North Road and the other Sea View. Both were later re-named Percy Road. (see 1920 OS map)

None of the houses had inside toilets or running water. The toilets were earth closets situated in a small stone building opposite the dwelling, with a low-level hatch to make emptying easier. The toilet waste would be covered in ashes from the household fire and collected weekly by a workman who would throw the excrement onto the back of a horse-driven cart to be taken away to be used as manure on the fields. Mr Kenneth Willcox, 91 years old and probably the second eldest original resident in the village in 2020, could recall two waste dumps, known as 'the mucks'. One was east of Lough's South East Farm and the second was on a section of land above where Colliers' Close was later built, where the small enclave of Fairfield View is presently located.

Colliers' Close, where Mr Willcox lived with his parents and family as a boy, had only two standpipes for the whole estate in the 1930s. Water was run from a massive, former ship-boiler, also situated near the mucks. This boiler was fed with water piped from a reservoir at the Beacon. Every house had a rain barrel for collecting water, which was used for bathing and washing. When necessary in dry weather, additional water would be collected from the Tylaw Burn which flowed in the field near his parents' house.

In the original village, around the church, residents drew their water from one of three pants situated near their homes.

West End Pant   North Side Pant   Percy Road Pant

Water Pants

The three pants in Shilbottle were all erected in 1868 by the Duke of Northumberland and provided the water source for the original village which was built around mediaeval common land. The West End Pant is Grade II listed. It was built of tooled, squared stone. The original tap has been replaced.

The North Side Pant is also listed. It is made of granite and sandstone, with a single step base and moulded plinth, with plain angle pilasters. The front panel has a bowl with bronze bucket-rest bars with an arched panel behind, made of polished pink granite. The small date tablet is above the panel. The top is moulded cornice with a swept dome.

The third pant is not listed and can be found midway along Percy Road at the foot of the pathway leading to the cemetery.

A fourth, less obvious, spring-water outlet is located off South Side, 100 yards east of the Farriers Arms. There was also a water pump on Middle Road

Middle Road Pump with the author's father in 1982.

Expansion of the village.

In 1925 and 1926 nine former army huts were transported from Alnwick for use by the men sinking the Grange Pit. The huts had three bedrooms, a living room, a large back kitchen and a bathroom with toilet. Each hut had an extensive garden. Two further huts were placed at the end of Sea View on Grange Road hill. When the wooden huts were condemned in the late 1950s, one was retained briefly for community use and first aid training. When this ended the huts were removed and towards the latter part of the 20th century, private bungalows were built on the vacated ground.

When the Grange Pit was being sunk, the colliery officials' houses were also being built. These were situated on the most easterly end of Grange Road on the hillside leading to Woodhouse Farm and the site of the colliery. The largest of the houses was in South View, at the top of the hill and was for the under-manager.

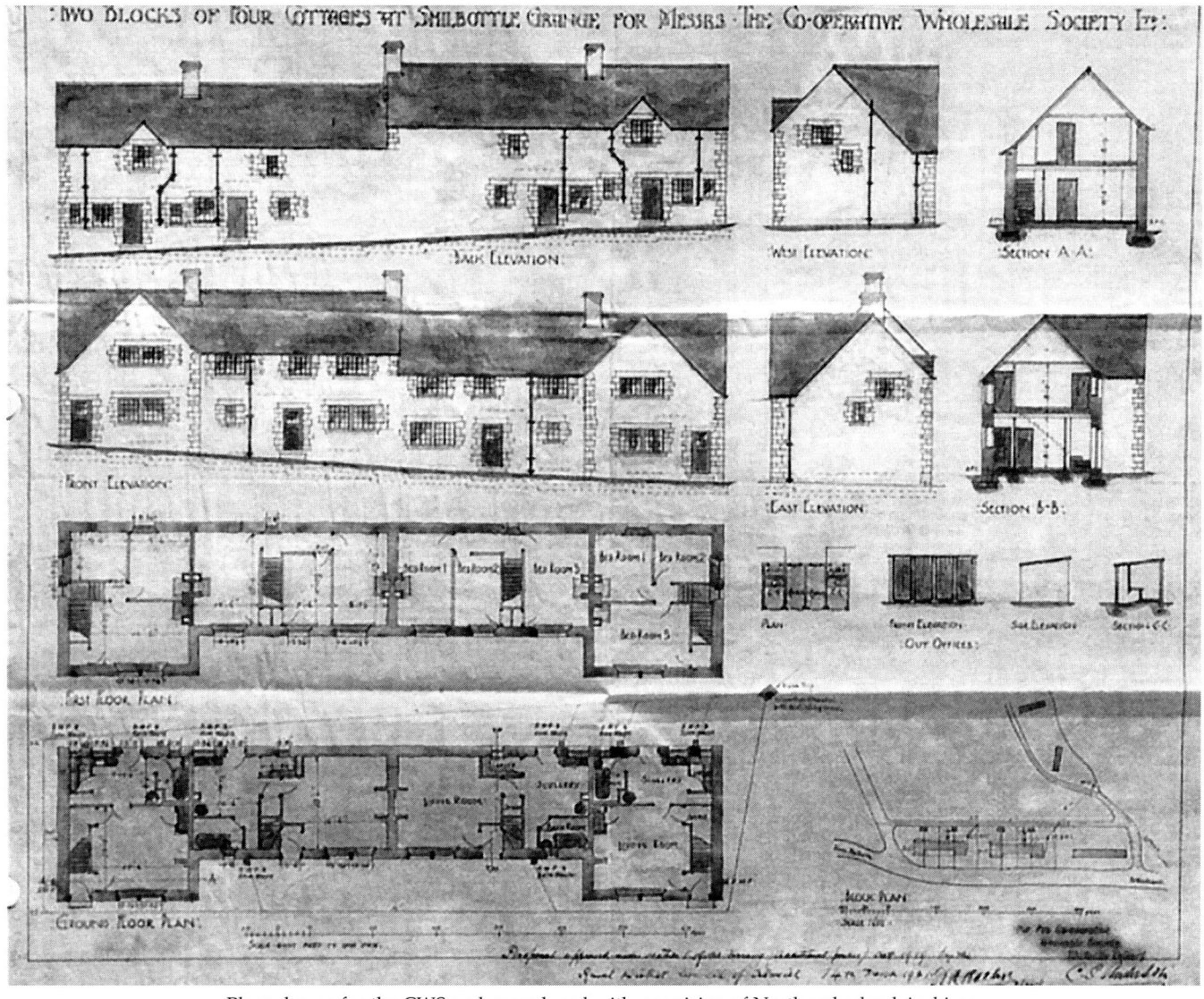

Plans drawn for the CWS and reproduced with permision of Northumberland Archives.

Unlike the plans above, there were only three houses in South View. Three other blocks of four houses were built on the hill. These were Castle View, Coquet View and Sea View.

Soon after the building of the stone 'View' houses, the concrete-block houses for the miners of the recently sunk Grange Pit were built and given the name 'Colliers' Close', although more commonly they were known as 'The Concretes.' A report written for the C.W.S. on 17th March 1926, referring to these concrete block houses, states:

> The houses – Garden City style (of which there are 40) – called Colliers' Close from the name of a field on an old map, sit close to a recreation field of 8 acres, for football and quoits, with a children's corner with swings – costing about £120 to fix up.

At this time the 24 bungalows of Hawthorn Terrace and the fourteen of Garden Terrace were constructed. As housing needs became more acute, with the influx of new miners, brick houses were built to the southeast of the village, in what became known as 'Shilbottle Grange.' The first houses to go up were nineteen semi-detached council properties in Grange Road early in the 1920s. Kiln Lonnen followed with a further thirteenhouses.

At this time the CWS owned 29 houses at Bilton Banks and a cottage as well as 136 houses in Shilbottle including a large detached house for the colliery manager and a caretaker's house at the Grange Colliery.

The 30 dwellings for Fallodon Avenue were constructed in Shilbottle in the 1930s. The majority of these houses were built on a spacious portion of land. Some had gardens of up to 40 yards in length. Except for six semi-detached bungalows, in what became known as *the keyhole* off Fallodon Avenue, they were of similar design. They had three small bedrooms, a bathroom with toilet on the upper floor, a large kitchen, coal store at the rear, a pantry area near the entrance door, and a single living room downstairs.

The next 34 houses to be built in 1948 were Lee Avenue, named after the Reverend Percy Lee: *A devout and respected parson who had served the Parish as vicar for twenty six years.*

Lee Avenue was extended in the 1960s to provide a total of 100 dwellings. The builders for the second phase were 'Slowthers of Alnmouth'.

In the late 1920s, 21 houses were built for workers on Beacon Road at Hampeth, with a further eight bungalows at Elmfield Terrace close to Whittle's drift-mine's entrance. The tarmac road surface approaching Elmfield Road from Shilbottle is unusually bordered on each side by granite cobbles, which were laid in the 1920s to aid horses drawing coal carts from the colliery to climb the steep hill leading towards the Beacon and Shilbottle.

The Prefabs

In 1949 the field to the north of the officials' houses leading down Grange Road, which had been retained by the colliery for exercising the horses used to haul the coal delivery and 'midden clearing' carts, was designated suitable for the erection of prefabricated houses. The estate had 25 detached bungalows and became known as Beech Estate. The prefabricated bungalows have since been converted into more substantial brick built and tiled roof dwellings.

The village of Shilbottle also expanded westwards with the influx of incomers into the estate of Farne View which was built between 1952 and 1953 specifically for miners relocating after their village mines closed in Cumberland and Scotland.

In the ten years since the millennium, more, private housing has been erected in the village, opposite Percy Road and west of the church of St. James' towards Farne View.

Elevated image showing the houses of The Square bottom left, the roof of George Nyberg's fish and chip shop partially obscured by the trees to the right, the post office on the left of Grange Road, and beyond, the houses of Lee Avenue in the near background, The Grange houses and in the far background the cluster of houses forming the dwellings in the middle of the village. *courtesy of Elisabeth Haddow*

Fallodon Avenue in the snow. *Keith Wilson collection*

Sections of prefabricated houses being manouvered into place during assembly. *Author's collection*

Shops and Commercial Outlets

The Butcher's.

At the turn of the 20th century, the village butcher's shop was in Church Row. It was part of Dick Taylor's home. The slaughterhouse was at the rear of the property. Dick Taylor had served his time as a butcher at Benton, Newcastle upon Tyne. Lillian, Dick Taylor's daughter and her husband Denys, the Reverend Hume's son, lived next door to the butchers. Dick Taylor rented a Glebe field at Hitchcroft and when a beast was to be slaughtered, it was walked a mile east down the road into the village. It was common to slaughter one cow and four sheep per week, these additional animals (usually reared by Taylor's farmer relatives at Seaton Point, along the coast and north of Alnmouth) were most often bought at Alnwick Mart and also walked back to the village.

Villagers called at the butcher's shop or bought from Taylor's travelling shop as he toured Shilbottle and surrounding hamlets. From the 1940s Turnbull's butchers from Alnwick and Moore's from Warkworth came into the village to sell their meat from a travelling shop.

Joe Straughan and Dick Taylor outside Dick's butcher's shop with his Austin van.
Ann Baston collection

Public Houses

Shilbottle had three public houses; Percy Arms, near the Methodist Chapel in the West End, The Farriers Arms on South Side, and the Black Swan Inn, on roughly the site of the Parish Room.

In 1855, 1858, 1861 – 1891 the Brown family were licensees of the Percy Arms. During the same period the Muers family were running the Farriers Arms.

The 1827 *Parson & White Directory* displayed on the Northumberland Communities site for Printed Material, Shilbottle, shows William Lumsdon to be victualler of The Turks Head in Shilbottle which is not referred to in other literature about Shilbottle nor shown on any maps. The entry could be wrong or the entry could possibly relate to The Turk's Head in Alnwick, with the victualler residing in Shilbottle.

Census data and directory records show that between at least 1841 – 1871, Joseph Wrigglesworth was publican/innkeeper of the Black Swan. Joseph was born in Shilbottle in 1810 and was one of eight children.

From 1913, The Farriers was the only inn/public house to survive

From the mid 1700s both the Farriers Arms and the attached smithy were tenanted by members of the Muers family, who held the licence for over 200 years. In 1860 the innkeeper was Margaret Muers, a widow with three sons, two of them blacksmiths. She had two daughters who were dress makers, one later becoming the post mistress. Margaret Muers died on 13th July, 1886, aged 83. Her son, Robert Muers immediately left the Percy Arms, returned to the Farriers Arms and became the licensee.

Robert was still licensee in 1891 and he was responsible for remodelling the Farriers Arms in 1894. He added upstairs bedroom accommodation, a large bar room which occupied the centre of the building on the ground floor and to the right of the main entrance. To the right of the main front entrance a comfortable 'select' room was added. An outside toilet was created and by then beer barrels were stored in the cellar.

Under the Muers, The Farriers Arms became a thriving hub for the village, catering for events such as the Shilbottle Feast Days, the Shilbottle Cycling Club Supper in 1895 and the Coronation Celebrations in 1911.

In 1943, Jane Ann Muers, widow of Thomas Muers and daughter in law of Robert Muers, retired as innkeeper of The Farriers. The inn and the attached smithy were sold by the executors of the late Duke of Northumberland, who was killed in the retreat to Dunkirk in 1940.

In 1964, following a publicised boycott by patrons who complained about the deteriorating facilities in the pub, major renovations were made to the old smithy to create a lounge, better seating and toilet facilities. Until 1990, the Percy Hunt, led by the Duke and Duchess of Northumberland, met there on Boxing Day. In April 2019 the east wing of the Farriers Arms was taken over by The Running Fox restaurant/cafe chain.

Post office in North Side. *Author's collection*

Joseph Straughan (1865-1947)

William Tate Straughan (1896-1984)

Reading Room

In the mid 1800s, a Reading Room was located at the Village Green end of Widows' Row. The manageress was Granny Corbett, who inspired countless young people with a 'devotion to 'checkers' or 'draughts. The 'men' were made of mahogany; square for the black and round for the white.

The Post Office

Originally the school master, at the Church of England School, was also the postmaster. The post office was later moved to North Side.

In the 20th century the post office was moved to a detached house in a more central location 400 yards east of St. James' Church. The postmaster then was Bob Clark. When he moved on in the 1950s, the role was taken over by the Marr family, who many years later moved to Warkworth Station. During their ownership Mrs Marr also sold home bakery, cooked ham, bacon and groceries.

Straughan's Carting

Joseph Straughan had a carting business with stables and yard towards Denecroft/Hitchroft.

The Green Hut

The Green Hut was an insignificant wooden hut located at the corner of Percy Road and Grange Road a few yards from St. James' Church. It was built in the early 1900s by Billy Robertson and the local policeman PC Beard. They sank a 200 gallon petrol tank at the front of the hut. The hut had no running water and the heating of only two paraffin stoves. Much later, health and safety regulations would have quickly closed the business, but then it prospered.

The Green Hut sold groceries, tobacco, books, stationery, paraffin, petrol, cycle and motor cycle parts, confectionary and small household goods. Only licensed newsagents were allowed to sell

newspapers and that was the mainstay of Billy Robertson's business which he ran with his wife Frankie.

Her sisters Gertie and Maggie went around the village on Fridays to collect paper money that was due. In 1958 Billy and Ray moved from their house opposite the Council School to Arden House, around the corner from the Green Hut on Percy Road, which they built as a dwelling and grocery shop.

Throughout, the years, except for national service, their son Ivan worked in the Green Hut. Children from the village went for their 'mix-up' of sweets ranging from half pence to five pence, self selected by the youngsters themselves and put into a paper bag. Old men would sit chatting on the two seats opposite the hut, beneath the church at the corner of Percy Road. They would wander across to the Green Hut to buy their 'baccy sticks' of the same type they had bought for chewing down the mine, to keep their mouths moist among the coal dust.

Throughout the year, the Green Hut opened at 5.30 am and closed 12 hours later, except for Sundays which was their busiest day, because all the other shops were closed. When business on the premises ended at noon, Ray, with an eye for business, would call at the Working Men's Club with boxes of 'Black Magic' and 'Milk Tray' for the men to buy and take home to their wives at closing time.'

Prior to 'Guy Fawkes night' the shop would have a corner dedicated to the storage of 'Standard' fireworks; and before Christmas the hut was an 'Aladdin's Cave' of board games, glittery Chrismas cards and annuals for the children – *The Bunty*,

Top: The Green Hut at the corner of Percy Road and Grange Road
Centre: The Green Hut.
Bottom: Billy Robertson with morning papers for the Green Hut, collected from Warkworth Station.

The Judy, *The Broons* and *Oor Wullie*.

Anne Armstrong, remembering the Green Hut said,

> The first thing that comes to mind is the delicious smell that came from a combination of paraffin stoves burning, tobacco, chocolate, sweets, newspapers and magazines. ... I recall buying my PAN editon of 'Casino Royale' for 3/6d. If I didn't have the ready cash, the Robertson family would put it away for me until I did. Taking advantage of this arrangement, I managed to read my way through Hammond Innes, Alistair Maclean and John Le Carre.
>
> I realise what a debt we villagers owed the Green Hut and the Robertson family – and what tremendous service they gave us for so many years.

The Green Hut closed on New Year's Eve 1985 and was demolished in 1997.

The corner on which the hut stood has been officially named 'Green Hut Corner', once with a plaque on the wall where the hut was located, until it was stolen.

Ivan and his wife Sheila woking in the Green Hut.

The site has been made into a commemorative garden to remember miners killed in Shilbottle Colliery and those Shilbottle servicemen killed in various military conflicts over the last century.

Fish Shop

Shilbottle's first fish and chip shop was opened by George Nyberg just after the Second World War. George had been accidentally shot by a recruit soldier using a Bren gun and was later given financial compensation by the Ministry of Defence which he used to start his business. Which was conducted in the front room of Nyberg's small detached house, on the bend of the road, a few yards east of Robertson's Green Hut. For decades it served villagers quality fish and chips take-away meals wrapped in grease-proof paper and recently read newspapers.

A clean-water spring surfaced outside George Nyberg's house and miners travelling to the Grange Pit would regularly stop there to fill their water bottles.*

The Co-operative Store

At the beginning of the 20th century, the Co-operative Wholesale Society opened a large wooden hut, as a shop, on Grange Road. The manager lived immediately next door in the largest brick house on that road. It served the community for ten or more years.

Roy Inglis sitting on the wall of the Co-op.

Roy Inglis collection

---

* Information provided by Mr Kenneth Willcox (aged 91) who was a life-long friend of Harry, Mr Nyberg's son. The information in the sub-chapter on the Co-operative store was provided by Mrs Irene Marshall.

On 11th June 1920 an agreement was signed between the 'Co-operative Society Limited, Manchester and Amble Co-operative Society for the sale of land, originally set aside for two houses, for the construction of a stone building to be used as a grocery and drapery store, in Shilbottle, at a cost of at least £2,000'. Shilbottle's purpose-built Co-operative store, in the centre of the image opposite, was opened in 1925 as part of Amble Co-operative Society Limited.

The Co-op can be seen in the centre of the photograph. It was a two storey stone, detached building situated beneath the officials' houses of South View. It was in line with the three other stone-built blocks of officials' houses of Castle View, Coquet View and Sea View, on Grange Road leading towards the Grange Colliery. In its heyday the co-op sold nearly everything needed for home and work. The upstairs stocked lino tiles, rugs, nappies, suitcases, pick axes, wellingtons, bit boots, shoes* and more, which were strung from the ceiling beside various other items of hardware. Downstairs they sold groceries, dairy product, cigarettes, and bacon cut on the premises. Butter too was cut from a block. Sugar and flour were measured from sacks. Milk was delivered to the dairy at the back of the premises, where dried pulses were stored in sacks, which were later given to customers and used by them as the backing for 'proggy' and 'clooty/clicky' mats. Milk coupons were sold and used for the purchase of milk.

Andy Hall was the milkman who took deliveries to outlying areas. He was succeeded by John Hetherington and later Mr Davies.

Every family had a dividend number which in due course accumulated to give them benefits. Orders were taken by the staff, of which there were eleven or twelve, some of whom went out to customers to note their requirements. Deliveries were made fortnightly to hamlets and houses in the surrounding countryside.

The store would buy and resell blackberries picked by children, and occasionally mushrooms collected from the fields.

From the 1950 the staff included:

Jimmy Pringle (manager), Tom Slater (under-manager, manager after 1960) store staff included: Christine Agnew, Brian Egdell, Jimmy Ferguson, Vivian Haddow, Jack Hayes, Shirley Hindhaugh, Evelyn James, Pat Lough (née Snowball), Irene Marshall (née Brand), Veda Micheson, Alison Ogle, Billy Ogle, Brian Rennison, Edna Snaith, Winnie Thompson, Joyce Tweedy and Irene Wheaden.

Women were employed only if they were single. This rule changed in 1966.

If the Co-op could not supply what customers wanted, they would be sent on to the Cooperatives

The Co-op building on the left of the photograph.
courtesy Keith Wilson

Wholesale warehouse in Newcastle where there was always a greater range of goods; or by arrangement the customer's requirements would be sent to the store for collection.

When Presto Supermarket opened in Ashington, and car ownership increased, the Co-op in Shilbottle started to decline. It closed in 1973 and was sold to Hubb Hire of Ellington. The upper floor was converted into residential flats and later the ground floor was let out to a hairdresser until 1983 when M & I Marshall took it over as a fireplace store. This closed in 1989 when the building was totally converted into residential property.

Throughout the years the Amble Co-op's travelling baker's van came into the village and the Allans from Red Row toured the lanes selling paraffin, candles and household goods.

Cottage Commerce

Between 1921 and 1922 Jean Hall's grandmother kept a little shop from which she sold sweets and cigarettes to contract workers. In the 1950s, Mrs Julia Chrisp who lived at No. 1, Garden Terrace, kept a range of flavoured mineral waters, supplied to her by Waters and Robson of Morpeth under a kitchen table in her scullery. She sold this 'pop' to villagers for a small profit.

Recent shops and food outlets.

Towards the end of the 20th century when the Green Hut closed, Ivan Robertson opened a grocery and fish and chip shop in a new building opposite Percy Road and adjacent to The Square. The post office, then

---

* The Reverend Pat Rennison, Ordained Local Minister and life-long resident of Shilbottle, recalled that shoes could be taken away on a trial basis, provided they were paid for the next day if they proved suitable.

owned by Arthur and Elizabeth Haddow, sold greeting cards, stationery and small items of confectionery. Next to the Working Men's Club a Spar grocery store was opened. This later became a village initiative and subsequently moved to the west end of the club, where there is also, at the time of writing, a pharmacy. A skills centre in the Club was established and opened by Anne, The Princess Royal, in 2000.

In 1982 after two years in the construction, 'The Carrib Northumbria' restaurant, behind Percy Cottage, opened. For nine years it was an important hub for villagers, providing among other things, a special Sunday lunch for village pensioners. It also provided a welcome reception for the French visitors who came to the village as part of the *Amicale* exchange.

The 'Carrib' closed in 1991 until a separate restaurant the 'Bengal Cottage' emerged. In 2015 the building was refurbished and reopened as 'Lal Khazana' restaurant.

Shilbottle's Working Men's Club

Early in 1939 a general meeting was called, following 200 signatures on a petition to establish a working men's club in Shilbottle, and on 29th May a Committee and officials were elected. The chairman, Mr F. J. MacDonald found a suitable site for a club house but the Second World War delayed development until a meeting on 8th September 1945, under the chairmanship of Mr George Eastham rekindled interest. His secretary was Mr Tommy Cook.

Land had been offered by the C.W.S. and was leased in February 1946. For £300 a large wooden hut was purchased with a loan from the Co-op. In February 1947 the club employed their first steward, Mr McLean on a weekly wage of £6 10s. 0d. The official opening was on 19th July, 1947 and as a special concession, 'members were allowed to bring their wives'.

As interest blossomed and applications to become members of the club increased it was agreed to purchase the freehold of the land from the landlords to build a new club with concert room. In 1951 Mr Tommy Ogle N.U.M. branch secretary backed a proposal to build a new social club officially opened in November 1955. The club was further extended to include a lounge in 1960 and as it continued to prosper the debts for the land and building costs were soon paid off.

The boom time for the club came to an end when the mines closed and within a few years the new – lounge was mothballed and later leased to the Village Action Group.

During its heyday the concert room of the Shilbottle Club was packed on a Saturday evening as miners and their wives played bingo prior to the dancing starting.

Each weekend the club committee would arrange singers and musicians to entertain the patrons. One local man, who toured the clubs as a singer at this time assumed the stage name of 'Happy Gay.'

The committee organised an annual Leek Show and the steward's wife made leek broth for patrons on the Sunday evening, from the vegetables deemed unsuitable for entry to the show.

The Village Magazine

In 1947 two young Shilbottle lads, Don Ogle and Alan Egdell began writing and publishing *The Beacon* magazine for the village.

They were constantly on the lookout for interesting stories. In July 1948 they reported that the new prefabs, to be called Beech Estate, were nearing completion. In the same issue they recorded that Frank Hedley scored 111 runs against Rock (his first century) and had added further wickets to his annual score bringing it to 56. Alan Egdell wrote a lengthy piece entitled *How to look for birds eggs*. He proceeded by suggesting caution: *Don't upset the adult birds ... never take more than one egg*, and never *take one that was due to be hatched*. Their publications incorporated local items of interest namely that *Dennis James and Esther Stewart, ... pupils of*

THE BEACON

Editor: DON OGLE   Sub-Editor: ALAN EGDELL

Vol. II   NOVEMBER 1947   No. 1

Editorial

This issue we commence Volume II. It is my wish that this volume goes through as well as the last. We have progressed slowly with Volume I, but it is a satisfactory thing to progress even a little and slowly than not at all. With this new volume I hope to make still further progress.

The glories of the summer are now but a memory, and autumn, in all its sad beauty, is with us. The birds of hedge and field, with the fear of the coming months of hunger upon them, are gorging themselves with the wild fruits of the season. The squirrels are very busy laying in their little stores, while other animals of the wild are searching for suitable winter quarters. Preparations for the winter are well in hand.

It may interest readers who went on the trip to Gretna Green to know the following: The original Gretna Hall marriage register, containing 2,000 entries of runaway weddings celebrated there since 1825 has been bequeathed to the county library at Dumfries by Miss M. C. Smith, of Wyseby, Kirtle Bridge.

Don Ogle

The register was bought by Miss Smith for more than £1,000, and she stipulated that it must be left for 10 years with Mrs. M. Macintosh, present owner of Gretna Hall.

I mentioned last month about our starting a fund for Alnwick Infirmary. We organised a dance for October 24th to help start us away with this. In due course I hope to be able to make known how we intend to utilise this fund for the benefit of the infirmary.

In conclusion, may I once again ask for more articles and a wider sale of our magazine.

DON OGLE.

Miss Margery Stewart ... had been successful in their Royal College of Music examinations in Newcastle.

The bulk of *The Beacon* consisted of short chapters taken from popular novels. The October edition in 1947 had the final chapter from Rex Conway's *Queen of the Ice*; and the November edition featured *Knocking Sense into Marwood*, by Colin Milne.

The January 1948 edition of *The Beacon* contained useful household hints: *The importance of keeping your hair brush scrupulously clean ...* adding tips like ... *Remove loose hair after brushing ... and wash the bristles in water with a spoonful of ammonia mixed with water.* There was also a sentence in the January edition suggesting that *a little turpentine will help freshen up the uppers of suede shoes.*

The two lads provided a useful public service too. They included the full time-table for Ord's buses running from Alnwick to Shilbottle and return each day. Monday to Friday, the first bus left Alnwick at 6.50 am for the 20 minute journey; the last bus returned to Alnwick at 11 pm. On Saturdays the morning run was the same but the last bus in the evening left for Alnwick at 11.30 pm. The driver had a long lie in on a Sunday morning; the first bus to Shilbottle left Alnwick at 11 am and the last in the evening returned at 10.45 pm.

The Parish Magazine

St. James' Church has produced a magazine for the parish since 1901. It was always a church and community publication with a wide circulation. In 1960 its name was changed to *The Scallop Shell* the scallop being the emblem of St. James. The magazine is issued ten times per year and reflects church activities across the parish. In 2020 *The Scallop Shell* won a National Competition for a magazine of its type.

Charlie Grant, the village handyman outside his shed.
Jacqueline Foster (née Grant) collection

The Village Handyman

Charlie Grant, a Scotsman from Elgin, met Connie his 'wife to be', whilst serving in the RAF during the war and billeted in Shilbottle. He married Connie in 1946 at Shilbottle and had a variety of jobs around the village – among them window cleaner, postman and joiner. He was later employed by the NCB to maintain the colliery houses. Whilst so employed the NCB constructed a large hut on the spare ground close to the prefab he, his wife and daughter, Jacqueline occupied in Beech Estate. His workshop was known around the village as 'Charlie's Shed.'

Transport

Tommy Ord's bus would transport workers from Shilbottle, and pupils who had secured places at the Duke, Duchess and Convent schools, to Alnwick each weekday morning.

On Saturday mornings, three early buses were often provided to take residents to Alnwick for their weekly shopping. The last bus home on Saturdays was always crowded.

Tommy Ord's bus, in Alnwick Market Place.

Shilbottle's most serious bus accident.

On 1st March 1965 28 children from the County School were being taken from Shilbottle to Alnwick for swimming lessons in one of Craigs of Amble's buses driven by Mr Derek Farr of East Chevington. The roads were very frosty and the bus skidded on the approach to the Cawledge Bridge nearest Alnwick. It collided with the bridge wall on the east side of the road demolished 20 feet of the stone parapet, went though it and landed upside down 30 feet below. It was partially submerged in the Cawledge Burn and wedged between the banks of the ravine. One student was supported in the water, by Mr Bob Mather, a local driving instructor. He came across the accident, while fire service personnel were busy using cutting gear to release some of the injured.

A shuttle service of ambulances subsequently conveyed the injured children and their teacher, Miss Janice Hill, to Alnwick Infirmary. There, five local doctors rushed to the hospital to help tend to the injured. Several young pupils were badly hurt including Hilary Hudson, who sustained a fractured skull and brain injuries; Edwin Swordy who lost sight in his right eye and fractures to his leg and wrist; Janice Hill who broke a collar bone; and Gary Prentice who was concussed and seriously shocked. These five, were later transferred from Alnwick Infirmary for treatment at Newcastle's General Hospital.

The bus driver Mr Farr and Edwin Swordy were subsequently transferred to the Royal Victoria Hospital.

Five boys, also in a state of shock and covered in blood, escaped from the bus and ran off towards Shilbottle. These included Geoffrey Grey, Paul Willcox and Richard Snaith. They sought help at Townfoot Farm and they too were taken by ambulance to Alnwick Infirmary. Paul Willcox had sustained a broken nose and substantial laceration to his head; Richard Snaith had severe bruising to his back. Paul and Richard, along with Susan Ogle, Judith Casson and Ann Inglis who had concussion, were detained overnight in Alnwick Infirmary.

The fathers' of the seriously injured children were called out of the pit to attend to their children.

The other boys involved in the accident were Kenneth Boyd, David Brewis, Trevor Haddow, Edwin Harle, Derek Hope, Tony Jackson, Malcolm Tailford, David Thompson, Melvyn Watson and David Whitworth. The other girls included Yvonne Barren, Veronica Patterson, Helen Snowball, Christine Taylor and Carol Watson.

It was considered a miracle that no one had lost their life.

Photographs of the Shilbottle bus accident. From the *Northumberland Gazette* 5th March 1965. with permission of Northumberland Archives NRO 06994-18-25

Sport and Other Pastimes

Upper: Shilbottle's Alnwick Wednesday League team in the 1902 – 03 season.
Lower: The youngsters who won the Amble and District School League in the 1909 – 10 season.
Author's collection

The majority of recorded sporting activity in Shilbottle village has been by men and boys. However, whilst men have dominated in competive activities and team games, women and girls in the village have contributed greatly in creative, community-binding activites of huge social worth. Also, even in the male dominated activities like football and cricket, women have played a crucial part behind the scenes, making football strips, providing and serving teas and refreshments and of course standing on the edges of pitches and grounds giving vocal support to their loved ones.

Most miners, who had spent 50 or more hours each week underground 'winning coal', enjoyed outdoor life when the opportunities arose and in Shilbottle association football played a key part in the village's history.

Organised football has taken part in the village ... since the early 1900s. Records indicate that a village team entered the North Northumberland Football League for the 1904 – 05 season and continued thereafter, except for the suspension of all competitions in Northumberland during the 1914-1918 war years.

In the mid 1920s with the opening of Shilbottle Grange Pit, an influx of miners added to the expanding population. In 1928 the Shilbottle Colliery Welfare Football Club came into being. It achieved its first success soon after, winning the North Northumberland League's Alnwick Infirmary Sanderson Cup in the 1930 – 1931 season.

---

*   Andrucci, Paul, *Memories of Shilbottle, Millennium Edition* (2000) p 98.

This is one of the earliest teams to play as Shilbottle F.C.

Paul Andrucci collection

Right: The Shilbottle AFC team which played in the North Northumberland League in the 1905 – 06 season.

Paul Andrucci collection

Below: Shilbottle Colliery Welfare FC prior to winning the Sanderson Cup.

Author's collection

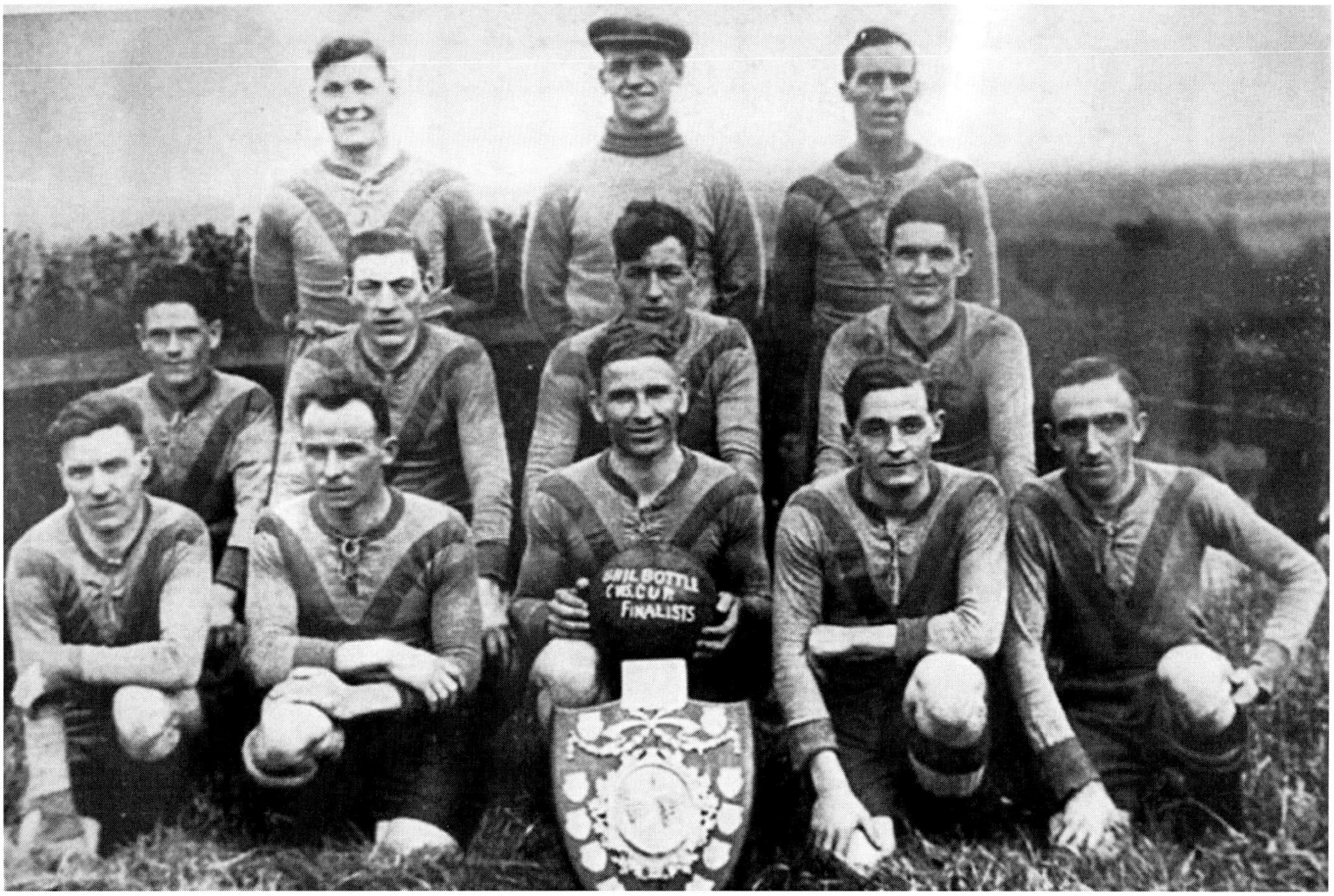

The Shilbottle team for the C.W.S. National Inter-Depot Cup Final was T.Pigg (goal keeper), H. Wood, A. Allan (full-backs) J. Maddern, T. Hodgson (Cap't), R. Slater (Half-backs), J. Brown, T. Bell, G. Batey, J. Green and A. Graham (forwards) *Paul Andrucci collection*

Probably Shilbottle's finest footballing achievement occurred in 1935, when a team from the village took on Silvertown at Woodford in London in the C.W.S. National Inter-Depot Cup Final, recorded in *Ourselves* the CWS magazine:

> Seven minutes to go; the score 1 -1; suddenly J. Brown received the ball just inside his own half. Running fast along the touch-line and keeping the ball under perfect control he worked his way towards the corner-flag, then centred. The ball went sailing towards the Silverton goal. J. Green at inside-left jumped into the air to meet the ball with his head and the next minute the ball was at the back of the net. Shilbottle had taken the lead.

The scorer of the winning goal was chaired off the field, shoulder high, by two of the travelling Shilbottle supporters.

The winning trophy was presented by the Director of the C.W.S. Mr G.A. McEwan, to Shilbottle's captain Tommy Hodgson. On return to Shilbottle Tommy Hodgson was carried shoulder high around the village, led by a drummer as the team made their way to the Farriers Arms

The team's success was recognised when their photograph was among a set of cigarette cards issued by Ardath Tobacco Co in 1936, featuring the football clubs of the North East Counties.

PHOTOCARDS

No. 10.

SHILBOTTLE FOOTBALL CLUB

Left to right, back row :—*T. Bell, H. Wood, T. Hodgson (Capt.), T. Pigg, G. Batey, R. Slater.* Front row :—*J. Brown, R. Clark, J. Cameron, J. Green, A. Graham.*

Formed in 1928, this club are members of the N. Northumberland League and finished 3rd for the Season 1935/36 and also won the C.W.S. Cup (All England) 1934/35. In Season 1930/31, were successful in sharing the Alnwick Infirmary Sanderson Cup, holding it for 6 months.

ARDATH TOBACCO CO: LTD: Manufacturers of STATE EXPRESS and ARDATH CIGARETTES

B

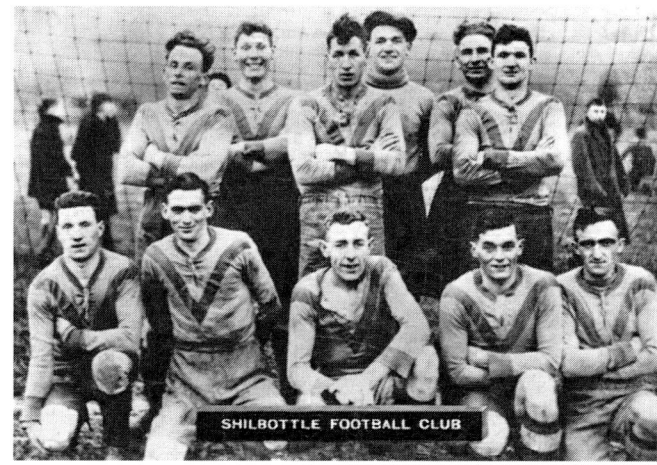

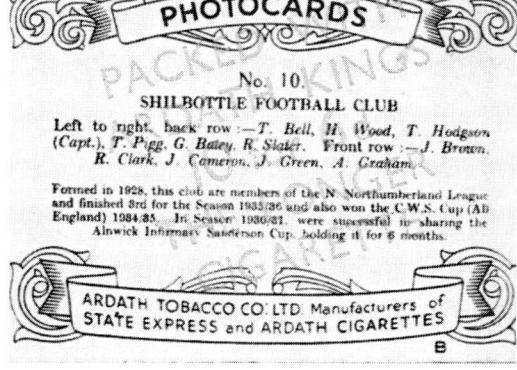

Front and back of the Ardath Photocard celebrating Shilbottle Football Club. *Author's collection*

In the post Second World War period Shilbottle's team entered the Northern Alliance Football League and returned to the North Northumberland League in the 1940s. Shilbottle's Northern Alliance League team: numbers 1 Bob Mather, 2 Tommy Tully, 3 George Luke, 4 George Slater, 5 Winker ? 6 Wally Snowdon, 7 Archie Stewart, 8 Jackie Luke, 9 Mick Wilson, 10 Ken Ord, 11 Mansy Tully.

Paul Andrucci collection

During the same decade Shilbottle Colliery Welfare Reserves won the North Northumberland League 1st Division Trophy, in the 1954 – 55 season.

Shilbottle Colliery Welfare Reserves cup-winning team.
Back left to right: Bobby York, Terry Weightman, Arthur Inglis, Tommy Morton, Andy Anderson, Jack Young
Front left to right: Gordon Black, Tommy Beattie, Jimmy Nolan, Billy Boyd, Michael Hewitt, (Mascot).

Paul Andrucci collection

Shilbottle Wanderers' Committee at their annual dinner in Shilbottle Working Men's Club in 1952. *Left to right:* Mr Charles Foster (Solicitor) Vice Chairman, Mr Joe Pattinson, Mrs Lough, Tom Lough (Chairman), Rev William Hume, Mr Ken Willcox (at the door), Mrs Longstaff and her husband, Mr Tommy Tully sitting at the extreme right.
The Wanderers achieved their first championship success in the 1957 – 1958 season. The following season they beat Newbiggin Colliery Welfare 6-5 in the Northumberland Aged Miners' Homes Cup.

Ken Wilcox collection

Sport and Other Pastimes

Left: Shilbottle Miner's Cup – Runners Up 1954-55 season

Back left to right: Tommy Tully, Ted Taylor, Alan Neale, Fred Watson, Jimmy Buglas, Alan Davison

Front left to right: Maurice Agnew, Jackie Coxford, Mansy Tully, George Mansfield, Ronnie Knox.

Paul Andrucci collection

Below: A football team from the late 1950s with players from 'the old pit' at Longdyke. George Knox is sitting at the extreme right.

Below: Shilbottle C.W.F.C. team's move into the Miners' Welfare League signalled the beginning of their most successful period in the club's history. They were league runners-up in the 1962-63 season; winners of the Aged Miners' Cup the same season; League Challenge Cup Winners the following season; and reached the final of the NFA Minor Cup in the 1964 -1965 season. The photograph shows the team that won the Berwick Cup away from home on 27th July, 1963.
Left to right: Dennis James, Keith Wilson, Ray Kelly, Bob Lazenby, Maurice Agnew, Doug Robson, Eddie Hope, Gordon Trustram, Chuck Brown, Jackie Hindhaugh, Malcolm Allan.

Keith Wilson collection

Players, committee members and lady supporters outside the Shilbottle Welfare Hall 1960. *Back row left to right*: Alf Weightman, Jackie Allison, George "Tishy" Elliott, Jimmy Weightman, Mansy Tully, Ken Willcox, Tommy Tully, Jimmy Tully. The ladies include Charlotte Punton, Mrs Pattison, Mrs Tully, Mrs Ball, Mrs Weightman. *Front row left to right*: John Wrigglesworth, Jackie Hindhaugh, Dennis James, Derek York, Raymond Tully, John Moore, Jackie Agnew, Tommy Muir, Terry Weightman, Stan Douglas, Henry "Chic" Brown, Thomas Easton, Keith Wilson, Ian James.

Keith Wilson's collection.

Jimmy Tully.

The Shilbottle team which won the NFA Minor Cup, played against Killingworth YPC Town at Whitley Park, Longbenton on 2nd May 2008.

Jimmy Tully managed the Shilbottle Football teams for 42 years.

During the 1960s in addition to the first team, the village fielded a reserve team which played in the North Northumberland League, and an under-18 team which played in the East Northumberland Junior League.

At the end of the 1967-68 season Jimmy Tully retired and during the following years as the mining industry went into decline, so did the Miners' Welfare League. Shilbottle's football club ceased for a number of years but in 1980 it reformed and joined the North Northumberland League Division 2 and also entered the Morpeth Sunday League.

The team won the N.N.L. Bilclough Cup in the 1987 – 88 season, were runners-up in the 1990 – 91 league, and won the league the following season. They were also runners up in two other cup finals: the Sanderson and Anderson Cups. The Sunday League brought continued success, their greatest achievement being run-away winners of the Second Division in the 2000 – 01 season.

After winning the NFA Minor Cup in 2008 there followed a period of about 10 years of trophies: in 2013/14 the NNL First Division championship, the NNL Lancaster/Laidler Cup, Stephen Carey Memorial Trophy and the Berwick Charities Cup. In the next season they won the Northern Alliance Second Division Championship, and in 2015/16 the Northern Alliance First Division Championship. The team won the NNL Robson Cup in 2017/18 which was their last game following the departure of players to higher grade clubs.

Cricket

Shilbottle Cricket Club was founded in 1927. At first they played their matches in what was known as Charlton's Field beneath the Farriers Arms. Subsequently the Welfare Ground became the venue for matches and a nissen hut became their pavilion. The Sporting Club in the village has a comprehensive display of photographs of successful teams;

Above: Shilbottle cricket team in the 1950s.
Back Row left to right: J Mitchison, A. Anderson, R. Hall, B. Dixon, W. McLean, L. Ogle.
Front Row left to right: H. Ternent, A. Inglis, N. Henderson, B. Billclough, T. Morton, A. Henderson.

Billy Hossain collection

Left: Shilbottle Welfare's Cricket eleven in the 1960s.
Back Row left to right: Ernie Riddle, Ronnie Ogle, Tom Pattinson, Brian Lough, Eric Rogerson
Sitting left to right: Henry Straker, Billy Hossain, Peter Edgell, Maurice Agnew, ?, Arthur Baston.

Billy Hossain collection

The winners of the Alnwick and District Vice President's Cup, played at Warkworth on 2nd September, 1979, against Guide Post, who were unbeaten in the league that season, and would carry on to win it. Guide Post also secured victory in the Tait 20 overs cup. They expected to beat Shilbottle in the 40 overs match, but the local team scored 151 for 9, bowling Guide Post out for 136.
Back row left to right: Stephen Robertson, Martin Inglis, Brian Lough, Ian Billanie, Dennis Allen, Peter Cameron.
Front Row left to right: Alan Black, Steve Johnson, Raymond Straker, Brian Darling, Henry Straker.

Raymond Straker collection

Ladies

In the 1970s the Tea Ladies struck out against the men at cricket in a fun match at the Welfare. The team shown comprised players from Shilbottle's sporting families.

Neither the score nor those responsible for making the tea that day are recorded, but the photograph shows the ladies' pride and is displayed among the men's photographs in the Sporting Club bar.

The Scout Movement

On 7th August 1909, the *Alnwick and County Gazette* reported that -

> Each centre of population is to have a Boy Scout committee who will have charge of the district and regulate the issue of Scout badges and find and approve suitable men to act as Scout Masters and keep a register of troops and patrols.

The first official scout camp was held on the links between Alnmouth and Warkworth with scouts from Warkworth, Amble, Shilbottle and Newton on the Moor being joined by a group from Liverpool. Mr Euan Sanderson of Eastfield Hall, Warkworth played a prominent part in that first camp. In November of the following year, following a meeting at St. Paul's Church in Alnwick, Major Widdrington of Newton was appointed president and Euan Sanderson secretary with Mr Munro of Abbey Lodge as assistant secretary. The first camp of the Alnwick and District Association was held at Birling North Field, near Warkworth on 12th November 1910. There were patrols and troops from Alnmouth and Lesbury, Amble, Eglingham, Felton, Glanton, Newton, Radcliffe and Shilbottle. Each day began with reveille at 7 am, followed by physical drill, breakfast, tent inspection, scoutcraft, bathing parade, dinner, free time, tea, scouting practices and games, supper and Last Post at 9.30 pm.

Back Row left to right: P. Lough, G. Straker, J. Allan, J. Inglis; *Middle Row left to right*: M. Jeffrey, R. Andrucci, D. Cameran, E. Straker, L. Straker; *Front Row left to right*: M. Billanie, F. Allan.
Paul Andrucci collection

Shilbottle Scout Troop 1925. *Billy McKnight collection*

Shilbottle Cub Pack 1928. *Carol Hope collection*

Pit Holidays

Before the time of package holidays, when Shilbottle colliery closed in July (subsequently August before reverting to July) several buses would take whole families to Butlin's Holiday Camps at Filey or Ayr. Other Shilbottle families, who either didn't have the finance or preferred community camping (perhaps following male members having experienced life under canvas through scouting), would take their ex-army tents to the south-side of Alnmouth at Buston, staying there sometimes from Easter until the schools returned at the beginning of September. The South-Side was known as the "Shilbottle Side" and the men would travel back to Shilbottle by bike for their work when their holidays were over, returning to their camp after work to join their wives and children who remained at the South Side to enjoy the relative peace and solitude of the seaside during the school holidays.

The travelling grocers and butchers journeyed to the 'Shilbottle Side' to maintain their business while the colliery village was mainly deserted during the pit holidays.

Reverend Pat Rennison recalled that often a 'Sea King' helicopter from nearby RAF Boulmer would do its practising over Buston Beach on Sunday afternoons. The campers would hold up a bottle of beer for the winch man to send down a rope for the beer to be passed up for the crew.'

The Inglis Family – their camping gear being loaded onto Uncle Norman Shell's wagon and at the beach, set for an extended stay – Cliffy and his dad Andy, with Rex their German Shepherd.

John Stewart
author's collection

Tommy Cook, John Stewart and Dickie Nicholson *c.* 1938.

Tommy Cook and Bob Knox at the 'Shilbottle Side' in the 1950s.

Sandra and Billy McKnight collection

Jimmy Hope manhandling his future mother-in-law, Gwen Inglis, assisted by Norman Shell at Buston Beach.

Left to right: Carol Inglis, Roy Inglis, Ron Patton, Cliffy Inglis, Maggie Thompson, Maureen Jobson, Hazel Thompson, Pat McCarthy.
Keith Wilson and Maureen Winn (Nee Jobson) collection

The above group includes Elwen Wilson, Maureen Jobson and Roy Inglis.

The Duke of Edinburgh's Award Scheme

In the late 1950s Northumberland County Council inaugurated a 'County Badge Scheme' for schools. The aim was to encourage young students to participate in outdoor expeditions, physical sports and activities and socially enriching experiences involving service to the community. It was virtually equivalent to the Duke of Edinburgh's Bronze Award. Many students who obtained the County Badge went on to complete the Silver and Gold badges and certificates of the Duke of Edinburgh's Award scheme. On the right are some of the first young people from Northumberland to obtain their awards at Holyrood Palace in Edinburgh in 1963. The head teacher of Amble Secondary School and Miss Valerie Tully, County Youth Organiser, are photographed with the former students from Amble Modern School; three are Shilbottle lads, the others lived in Amble.

Left to right: Dennis McBride, Miss Tully, head-teacher Frank Johnson, Keith Wilson (Shilbottle), Keith Armstrong, Jennifer Johnson, Barry Stewart and Colin Slater (both Shilbottle). *Author's collection*

The Pigeon Club

Scattered around the village, pigeon 'crees or duckets' were, and are, clearly evident in gardens and allotments; men and boys playing an active part in breeding sleek birds specifically for competitive flying. The authors of the Millennium edition of *Memories of Shilbottle* wrote: 'The Club continues to flourish with many men playing an active part' ... 'their birds being sent abroad on a regular basis.'

Other Social And Community Activities And Events.

The final paragraphs in *Memories of Shilbottle* pay tribute to the work carried out by a small group of researchers and gatherers of information which went into their commemorative publication. The publishers recorded snippets of detail about a whole range of social and community activities within the village including the following:

Shilbottle Women's Institute formed in 1928, with its successful choir.
The Flower Show, which began in 1934.
Shilbottle Over 60s Club with a history spanning 50 years.
Shilbottle Cub Scout Troop also with a half century history.
The Village Pantomime beginning in 1961.
The Shilbottle Mothers' Club which came into being in 1968.
The Bowling Club also formed in 1968 and met in the Welfare Hall.
Shilbottle's Jolly Girls formed mid 1970s.
Shilbottle's Garden Association, beginning in 1976.

British Red Cross

The chapter on mining in Shilbottle provides details of the number of fatalities in the Grange Pit during its period of operation. It also provides brief details of the number of serious injuries suffered by miners. There is also a photograph of senior managers from Longdyke Colliery at the Church of England School in the village in 1908, where

An example of underground training – Archie Inglis treating his son Andy helped by a colleague, with Bill Shepherd beside the stretcher looking on. *Sandra McKnight collection*

they were undertaking first aid training. Knowledge of how to assist injured workmen and provide potentially life-saving assistance was important, and along with mine rescue techniques, first aid training became a requirement for deputies and overmen at most collieries.

Inter-colliery competitions took place and winners of regional competitions went on to compete at National level in London

Not only did team members succeed in such competitions they did good work in the village, training youngsters in first aid. Some gave up their annual holidays to organise and run holiday camps for handicapped and underprivileged children from Tyneside.

In 1956 John Stewart and Alan Henderson ran such a camp in the former Isolation Hospital at Rothbury in Northumberland.

The Shilbottle Colliery 'First Aid' Team John Stewart kneeling behind the cups. *Author's collection*

Above: A group of adult organisers, visiting speakers, junior Red Cross cadets and several of the boys with physical handicaps who were being looked after and given experiences away from their families and neighbourhoods on Tyneside. John Stewart is second from the right in the second back row, next to his son Brian. The author is second from the left in the front row.
Author's collection

Left: Some of Shilbottle's finest (including Fenwick Brabben) on duty at Ratcheuth Races, the point to point race course a couple of miles east of Alnwick.
Roy Inglis collection

Village Hall And Other Venues.

At the end of the First World War plans for a Memorial Hall went ahead and included the recommendation that:

> Sufficient land between Shilbottle and Woodhouse should be available to allow the Institute, a caretaker's cottage, and recreation ground for the Sports Club which will be connected with the Institute. In the latter building, the Committee intends there shall be a large hall, constructed to the bye-laws, in order that it may be used as a Picture Hall when not being used for a concert or a dance. In addition, there will be a billiard room, games room, reading room and library, and other rooms where meetings may be held. When one remembers that the estimated population of Shilbottle in the near future is 2,000 to 3,000, the needs of such a hall and recreation ground is obvious. It is also desirable to notice that the distance from Shilbottle to Alnwick is nearly four miles, and that this distance will not be lessened when the new colliery houses are built. Furthermore, the majority of the miners now living in Alnwick and the surrounding villages will then be residents of Shilbottle.

The Institute, when built, had a snooker table and a meeting room which was used by a visiting barber and various local groups including the WI. The caretaker's house adjoined the Institute.

The wedding reception party for Rhoda Turnbull to Alan Atkins early in the 1950s, outside the Curch Hut; with Dave Henderson's car strategically placed. *Julia Tweedy collection*

The Church Hut

Prior to the building of the Welfare Hall, St. James' Church paid for the erection of a wooden hut in 1921. The hut was situated in the field opposite the Miners Institute adjacent to The Crescent houses and was used for all manner of Church and social occasions, remaining in use until 1954.

A presentation tea in the Church Hut for Shilbottle Juniors Under 16 football team. They were winners of the North Northumberland Junior League Cup in 1948. Those known to be present: *Left back row*: 1, Laurie Ogle, 2, Bill (Hoggy) Harrison, 3, Henry Wilson, 4, Terry Weightman, 5, Bobby York, 6, Gordon Egdell; *Left front row*: 7, Tommy Swordy, 8, George Knox, 9, Dixon Snaith, 10, Bill Wintrip, 12, Ernie Rennison, 14, George Stokoe, *Left seated*: 16, Freddie Watson, 18, Jimmy Ball; *Top Table*: 19, Jim Stokoe (Under Manager), 20, Darsen Watson, 21, Mrs Stokoe (U/M's wife), *Right seated*: 27, Mrs Thompson (Farriers), 28, Maise Watson, 29, Peg Watson, *Right standing*: 30, Maggie Swordy, 31, Jean Wilson, 32, 'Darkie Watson, 33, Julie Swordy (now Tweedy). *Julia Tweedy collection*

Fun and Games

Shilbottle Colliery was unique among coal mines in allowing its workforce to have a week's holiday on full pay during the summer months. The miners took advantage of this leisure time to organise an annual Feast during which there were fancy dress competitions, games and sporting events. The *Memories of Shilbottle, Millennium Edition* book records some of the activities and includes several photographs of participants during the 1930s and succeeding years.

The report prepared by Vera Mallon, based on *The Alnwick Journal* of 1860, quotes sports and pleasures enjoyed by Shilbottle folk in the 19th century. These included horse racing, pitch and toss, cock fighting, greyhound racing, bowling, pigeon flying, cards, quoits and cycling. Miss Mallon's report mentions that in 1895 Shilbottle inaugurated a cycling club and held races around the village and Alnwick.

The refreshments after most sporting events were provided by the Muers family at the Farrier's Arms.

The Shilbottle Feast held in 1860 took place over two days:

> firstly at the Black Swan and the following day at the Percy Arms. There were horse and donkey racing and Shilbottle Percy Band played a choice selection of music during the day.
>
> Sports consisted of quoits, 150 yards foot race, hop step and jump, a 200 yards handicap foot race, a standing leap and a three legged race.
>
> The first horse race was held at Dean Moor near the Great North Road but later moved to a field near Whittle. The Shilbottle Hunt Cup and the Alnwick Hunt Cup were guided by Grand National Rules, but the ladies race for the Ladies' Purse and Pony Race were run off in heats.

The last Shilbottle horse races took place in 1888.

The Annual Floral, Horticultural and Industrial Society Exhibition

The exhibition was established in 1884 and had its 4th event in the Church School rooms on 1st August 1888. In addition to the display of vegetable produce -

> Beautiful quilts made a pleasing show, hanging full length around the school, and hearth rugs, though not so imposing were none the less attractive.

There were separate classes for cottagers, farmers, school children as well as an open class.

The Welfare Hall was built in the early 1960s. Dances were held there most Friday evenings; the bowls club used the premises for indoor carpet-bowls matches, the cricket club served their mid-match refreshments and a youth club was held in the premises over many years.

Tinker Weightman as Lord Mayor and 'a lady friend' setting aside their inhibitions to dress up for one of the competitions.

Jack 'Chippy' Wood being 'lofted' by two colleagues (one is Bob Trotter) after competing in one of the Feast's football matches during King George Vth's Jubilee celebrations. This was in 1935, not long before the King died.   *both Sadie Rennison collection*

Sport and Other Pastimes

Another two of Shilbottle's characters masquerading as dignitaries during the Shilbottle Feast of 1985: Lord Mayor (Jimmy Ternent) and Lady Mayoress (Mary Howes) in July 1985 – with Shilbottle Welfare Hall in the background.
Author's collection

Below left: Tommy Scott with the Duke of Northumberland at the Millennium Gala.
Keith Wilson collection.

Below right: Shilbottle's obstacle course being attempted during the Village's sports day in the Welfare Field. *Roy Inglis collection*

More scenes from the Millennium Gala organised by Reverend Mike Dixon together with members of the parish.
Keith Wilson collection

Arthur Hossain captured village life in the 1950s in his vernacular poem entitled *Back Then*, reprinted with his permission.

> Wi darned up socks and patched up shoes
> we all ran aroond in wee short troos.
> Scabby fingers n'd scuffed up knees
> it's watt yu got fo climbing trees.
> Hopscotch and muggies on the path;
> played knock and run for a laff.
> Footie was played wi owt wu cud kick
> An auld tin can wud de the trick.
> Towed wa bogies up church hill;
> charged back doon fo a thrill.
> Doon tu thu Callishes ticklin trout,
> We'd never admit we caught nowt.
> Went willickin in rock pools on the coast,
> Then back yem fo drippin on toast.

The end of the Welfare Hall

The Welfare Hall was burnt to the ground in 2008 following what was believed to be an electrical fault. Construction work on a new hall was started on the site in 2009.

Over 60s outing. *Julia Tweedy's collection*

The Welfare Hall ablaze in 2008. *courtesy Russell M. Stalker*

A Women's Institute trip to Redcar in 1953, including Peggy Ball, Florence Batey, Hazel Billanie, Edna Burton, Belle Casson, Mrs Chrisp, Mrs Easton, Bisset Gray, Mrs McKay, Betty McLean, , Mrs Morton, Winnie Straker, Olive Ternent and Mrs York.
Julia Tweedy collection

A letter from the Coal Industry Social Welfare Organisation – dated 26th May 1964. Attached to it are a National Union of Mineworkers' lapel badge commemorating the NUM's 100 years of service to miners from 1883.

More particularly the letter has a blazer badge attached, which was presented for services rendered during a Northumberland and Cumberland Inter-Divisional Athletics Festival held in Nottingham in 1964.

This was at a time when Shilbottle Colliery was producing high volumes of quality coal and had a respected workforce. The NUM Membership Card badge for 1977, for Mr Alan Allcorn of Shilbottle Branch, was issued, however, when Shilbottle Colliery was beginning to run into operational difficulties, and it would not be long before coal production was achieved via a link with Whittle Colliery, before both collieries were forced to close.

The Coal Industry Social Welfare Organisation (CISWO) still exists to help and improve the lives of former coal miners and their families by supporting independent mining charities to continue developing recreational and social facilities in local communities.

Image provided by Mrs Alcorn by way of Sheila Robertson

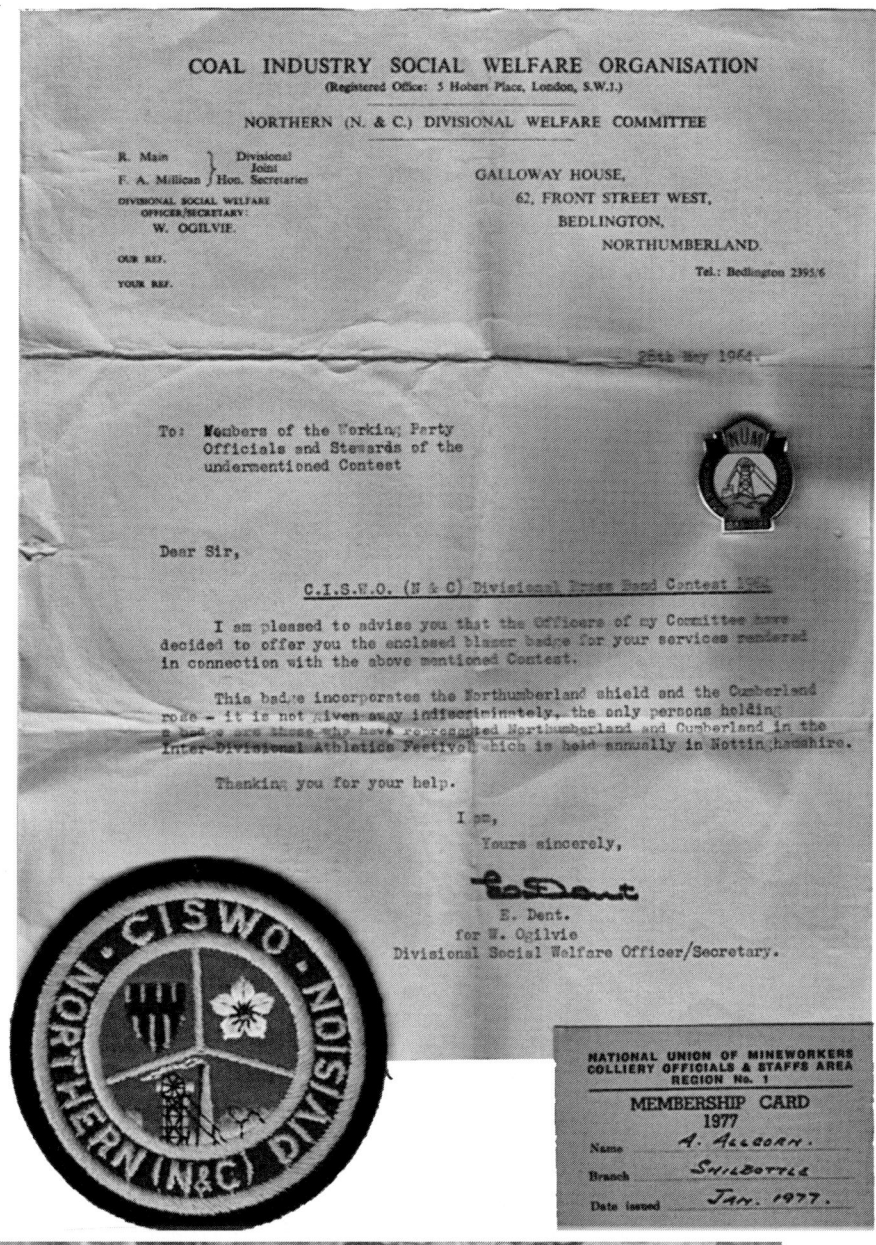

Simple pleasures in retirement, men resting on a bench at the foot of Middle Road, after a spot of gardening. Fenwick Brabben (senior), Mr Truman, Paddy the spaniel and Thomas Swordy in the 1950s.

Julia Tweedy collection

Entertainers

At weekends the Shilbottle Working Men's Club would be filled with miners and their wives, drinking with their workmates, playing Bingo and then dancing to Tommy Morton on the organ and Joe Knox on the drums.

Local talent like Ella Nicholson would take their opportunity to sing their favourite songs before giving way to the 'turn' for the night.

Right: Joe Knox and Tommy Morton playing in the Farrier's Arms in Shilbottle.

Centre: Shilbottle's Working Men's Club.

Jacqueline Foster collection

Bottom: The Club and a visiting brass band marking the opening of the new lounge.

John Robert Gay, a local lad from Hampeth was an accomplished performer who graced Shilbottle Club's stage, singing topical songs from the 'Hit Parade'. His stage name was 'Happy Gay' and he went on to have a successful, long lived career as a professional club performer.

Robert 'Happy Gay' with Billy 'Hogan Harrison'.

'Happy Gay' in his stage costume. *Billy Housain collection*

Robert Whitehead was born in Shilbottle. As a ten year old he began playing the accordion. His first gig, with his brother John on the drums, was at St. James' Church Garden Fete in 1963. His many achievements as a musician are mentioned in detail in the final chapter.

Robert at the door of 3 Grange Road, Shilbottle and in the 1970s.
Robert Whitehead collection

Scrambling

Usually on a Sunday afternoon motor cycle enthusiasts took part in off the road scrambling in the west of the village, on bikes which nowadays would be collectable vintages. The photograph on the right is believed to have been taken at Hazon, although the scrambling track at Whittle Quarry was also popular.

Above: Back row left to right: George Graham, Sandy Holden, Wallace Robson, John Mitchison, Davey Minery, Wilf Anderson, John Anderson. *Front row left to right*: Bill Wintrip, Willie Holden, Bill Rogers, Norman Mason, Robert Holden, Donald Snaith, George Darling. *Billy McKnight collection*

Left: Scrambling bikes with competition numbers. *Roy Inglis collection*

Jim Robertson in 1946 after competing in the Isle of Man TT races and his son Billy on his BSA Bantam racer in the late 1950s. *Roy Inglis collection*

Shilbottle's French Connection – *Amicale*

In 1963, the Mayor of Hery in Burgundy, (in the department of Yonne, near Auxerre, situated 80 miles from Paris and 90 miles from Dijon), asked an English resident called June Raynal and her French husband Jean to help establish a link with an English village.

June's uncle and aunt, Ossie and Sarah Patton had hosted June in Shilbottle village as a child. Later, after she finished university where she had studied French, June went to France. There, sometime later she met and married Frenchman, Jean. Meanwhile her aunt and uncle obtained permission from Shilbottle Parish Council to establish a friendship between the two villages which their niece knew so well.

June and Jean Raynal. *Anne Armstrong collection*

The then chairman of Shilbottle Parish Council, Mr W.A. Davison was heard to say,

> Our boys will be able to go to France now without being killed.

Hery and Shilbottle were considered to be perfect 'twinning' partners. There were close personal ties between the two communities; they were of similar size; both had rural and industrial populations; each had a primary school with their secondary school located in a nearby town; and the Davey-Bickford factory in Hery made detonators and explosives for use in mines and quarries.

Amicale (meaning friendly) was therefore born. Its objects were to:

> foster friendship and closer understanding between the two communities.

Initially membership fees of 2 shillings and 6 pence were collected in the 'bottom half' of Shilbottle village, but at a later date John Swordy, Joe Mackay and Ernie Tully, decided that if a person lived within the parish boundaries of Shilbottle they would automatically be a member of the association. Two associations with the same name, *Amicale* were set up in both villages on opposite sides of the Channel and the association came into being.

The first fifteen French visitors to Shilbottle, in the care of Monsieur Roger Balle, came in 1964. Their trip involved two train journeys in France, a short hop in the Paris Metro, a ferry from Calais to Dover, a train to London, taxis to Kings Cross, a train journey to Newcastle and then cars to their final destination in Shilbottle. The highlight of their visit was a trip down Shilbottle Colliery, an afternoon with their hosts in Warkworth around its castle and a Church Garden Party.

The group of visitors during their visit to the colliery. *Anne Armstrong collection*

Visitors and locals in the village.
Anne Armstrong collection

Anne Armstrong receiving a fountain pen from Monsieur Balle.
Anne Armstrong collection

Some of the visitors at the 'Shilbottle Side' beach (circa 1960) including Bobby and Colin Slater, Sandra Mather, Mary Patton, Keith Wilson and Cliffy Inglis.
Keith Wilson collection

Shilbottle visitors in Hery during the first visit to the village.
French visitors performing at Shilbottle Working Men's Club.
Anne Armstrong collection

At the Church Garden Party at St. James' Shilbottle Monsieur Balle presented a fountain pen, as first prize in a fancy dress competition to Miss Anne Armstrong who was dressed as Wilma Flintstone.

The year following the garden party a group from Shilbottle made a return visit to Hery.

While there, a treaty of friendship was signed by the Mayor, Monsieur Roger Guenue and countersigned by the then vice chairman of Shilbottle Parish Council Mr Terry Ryder. There was an act of remembrance at the village war memorial where Mr John Swordy, who had been one of the people instrumental in initiating and progressing *Amicale*, laid a wreath of poppies and presented a British Legion badge to Monsieur Maurice Hutton.

The following year the visitors from Hery were entertained at Shilbottle's Welfare Hall, and as a way of saying thank you, three of them performed at Shilbottle's Working Men's Club.

In 1967 the Shilbottle contingent set off by bus before taking a plane to Le Bourget airport in Paris. John Swordy, on the extreme right of the photograph, was by then chairman of the Association and Joyce Snaith, 4th left, was secretary.

Joyce officiated at the unveiling of a plaque on the wall of a house in the newly named Rue de Shilbottle.

Since those early days more than 50 exchanges have been made involving over 1,000 people.

Monsieur Balle is seen in the photographs below with Sarah Patton, June Raynal's aunt, cutting the Association's cake at the start of

its Silver Anniversary celebration, and next image, at the same celebration, shows the traditional exchange of gifts.

In each village the *Amicale* Association continues to hold social events. Many of them are shared with their new friends from over the Channel; the proceeds being used to fund further trips to their partner villages. Some family friendships have developed over three generations.

Notwithstanding the commitment of a few stalwarts, as people got older, the number of participants began to tail off. So, in 2008, five ladies from Shilbottle, (Irene Marshall, Pat Rennison, Yvonne Turner, June Nolan and Cynthia Mackay) flew to France to meet up with Sarah and Ronnie Patton who were already there staying with June and Jean Raynal. They kick-started the renewal of the Association. In 2013 50 years were celebrated.

Photographs from Ann Armstrong's collection.

Shilbottle's Military Record

Little is written or recorded about Shilbottle's involvement in military conflict in its very early days, but the castle at Alnwick and the walled town provide tangible evidence of the perceived need to provide security for the people of the town, at least from the 11th century when the castle was owned by Gilbert Tyson. There are hints too of the possibilities of a Saxon castle from an earlier time on the same site. It is known also that on a number of occasions Alnwick was sacked by the Scots and that in 1433 a licence was granted by Henry VI to enclose the town in walls with gated towers. The financial and physical burden for this fell on the town's burgesses and the town's people to accomplish.

Shilbottle, more isolated, open and vulnerable, only a few miles south-east of Alnwick, was obviously a potential target too as the fortified Pele Tower of the village bears witness. It is listed in manuscripts compiled for King Henry V.

Also, at this time it is known that the Border region was vulnerable to Anglo-Scottish Border Reivers.

The muster roll for Shilbottle in 1538 comprised 24 able men, lacking in equipment and described as *wantyng bothe horse and harness,* but who *'were available to repel raiders and Reivers.*

The *Schelbotell Muster Roll* of 1552 highlights the need for vigilance against raiders and specifies that

> the night watch was to be kept from Hithcroft in Shilbottle parish to Rugley in the Parish of Alnwick, by ten men, drawn from the townships of Shilbottle, Whittle, Sturton Grange, High Buston, Low Buston, Wooden and Bilton.

In his *History of Northumberland (vol 5),* J.C. Hodgson records that:

> On 11th June 1587 six Scotsmen from Teviotdale stole 8 horses, 320 yews, a further 19 mares, 16 sheep and other goods, and on 12th March 1589, on behalf of 9 of his tenant farmers the Duke of Northumberland prosecuted the men.

Men of the 7th Battalion Northumberland Fusiliers'.

There was definitely a need for vigilance against theft and attack. Despite this, by 1595 the Muster Roll had reduced to eleven able men. However, some of them were equipped with spears or petronels (an early type of gun).

The most recent and significant involvement of Shilbottle inhabitants, in military activities during modern times and about which most is known, was during the two world wars.

The First World War 1914 – 1918

The *Iron and Trades Review,* newspaper for 30th July 1915 reported that: *Whole regiments had been recruited from colliery districts ... and ... miners have contributed 250,000 men to the new armies.*

More than a third of the workforce at Longdyke Colliery, went to war. Joining battalions like the 7th of the Northumberland Fusiliers.

The 7th Battalion took part in the following battles:

Ypres in May 1915; the Somme offensive between July and November 1916; Arras between 9th and 16th May 1917; 3rd Battle for Arras (Passchendaele) between July

Trainee soldiers of the Northumberland Fusiliers in Alnwick Pastures at the beginning of the Second World War.
Sadie Rennison's collection

and November 1917; the first Somme between 21st March and 5th April 1918, and the second Somme from late August to early September 1918.

The Northumberland Fusiliers earned 67 battle honours including five Victoria Crosses but at a cost of 16,000 soldiers killed in action, with many thousands wounded.

The following young men, formerly resident in or associated with Shilbottle, did not return:

Robert Baxter, (Sergeant 1903) 1st/7th Battalion Northumberland Fusiliers, killed in action on 15th September 1916, aged 26. He was the son of Isabella Baxter and the late Robert Baxter and is commemorated on the Thiepval Memorial, Somme, France.

George William Buglass, (Private 203154) 1st Battalion Northumberland Fusiliers, killed in action on 3rd July, 1917. He was the son of Henry and Margaret Buglass of Bilton Banks and is buried in Hermes British Cemetery, Pas de Calais, France.

Thomas Heatley Charlton, (Rifleman 42834) 1st/8th Battalion West Yorkshire Regiment (Prince of Wales Own) was killed in action on 9th October, 1917 aged 30. He was the youngest son of the late Joseph and Phyllis Charlton of Hitchcroft, Shilbottle and husband of Jane Isabella Charlton of Elder Cottage, Shilbottle. He is commemorated at Tyne Cot Memorial.

William Henry Darling, (Private 2173) 1st/7th Battalion Northumberland Fusiliers was killed in action on 17th June 1916, aged 24. He was born in Shilbottle and enlisted in Alnwick. He was the son of Robert and Margaret Darling and is buried La Laiterie Military Cemetery, Heuvelland, West-Vlaanderen, Belgium.

Joseph John Dunn, (Probably Private 31572) 7th Battalion North Staffordshire Regiment, was killed in action on the 26th August, 1918 aged 20. He was the son of William and Mary Dunn, Newton on the Moor and is commemorated on the Tehran Memorial, Iran.

Robert Green, (Lance Corporal 5614) (20th Tyneside Scottish) Battalion, Northumberland Fusiliers, died on the 27th April, 1917 aged 27. He was the son of the late William Ternent Green and Mary Green and he is commemorated at Pas de Calais, France.

Joseph Robert Hall, (Corporal 235171) 26th (Tyneside Irish) Battalion Northumberland Fusiliers (previously served with the 7th Battalion). He was killed in action on 5th June 1917 and is commemorated at Arras Memorial, Pas de Calais, France.

Joseph Robert Hall

John Hindhaugh, (Private 38250) 26th (Tyneside Irish) Battalion, Northumberland Fusiliers, was wounded in action and died on 12th November, 1917 aged 31. He was the son of John and Ann Hindhaugh of Bilton and is buried in Bucquoy Road Cemetery, Ficheux, Pas de Calais, France.

George Slater, (Driver T4 091593) Army Service Corps died on 3rd October 1916 aged 25 years. He was the son of Margaret Jane Bell and William Slater. Driver Slater died in Graylingwell War Hospital in Chichester of osteomyelitis, complicated by sepsis and heart failure. He was buried in Shilbottle Cemetery in October 1916.

John Smails, (Private 36056) 1st/4th Battalion, Kings Own Yorkshire Light Infantry. He died of wounds suffered in action on 22nd April, 1918 and is buried in Etaples Military Cemetery, Pas de Calais, France.

William Watson Smails, (Private 2031) No 2 Company 1st/7th Battalion, Northumberland Fusiliers, was killed in action on 26th April, 1915, aged 29. He was the son of Joseph and Jane Ann Smails of Shilbottle and husband of Isabella. He is commemorated on Ypres (Menin Gate) Memorial, Ypres, Belgium.

James Joseph Thompson, (Private 38295) 22nd (Tyneside Scottish) Battalion, Northumberland Fusiliers died on 27th April, 1917. He is commemorated on the Arras Memorial, Pas de Calais, France.

First World War photograph including Shilbottle man, Jimmy Weightman in 1916.
Sadie Rennison collection

James Joseph Thompson

Alexander Jacob Tweedy, (Private 38301) 22nd (Tyneside Scottish) Battalion, Northumberland Fusiliers was killed in action on 18th November, 1917. He is buried at Wancourt British Cemetery, Pas de Calais, France.

Thomas Henry Weightman, (Private 290501) 1st/7th Battalion Northumberland Fusiliers, died 26th October, 1917, aged 25. He was the son of Mr & Mrs S. Weightman, 8 Sea View, Shilbottle. He is commemorated at Tyne Cot Memorial.

Bryan Broomfield Weightman, (Private 2238) 1st/7th Battalion Northumberland Fusiliers, was killed in action on 26th April, 1915. He is buried in Seaforth Cemetery, Cheddar Villa, Langemark-Poelkapelle, Belgium.

Robert George Weightman, (Private 290499) 1st/7th Battalion Northumberland Fusiliers, died 26th October, 1917 aged 25 years. He was the son of Robert George and Mary Weightman of Grange Colliery, and husband of Ellen of 6 Garden Terrace, Shilbottle. He is commemorated at Tyne Cot Memorial.

Thomas Weir, (Private 41420) 7th Battalion Leicester Regiment, was killed in action on 8th October 1918, aged 19. He was the son of Andrew and Elizabeth Weir, West Lodge, Newton on the Moor. He is buried in Prospect Hill Cemetery, Gouy, Aisne, France.

James John Wilson, (Private 290498) 1st/7th Battalion Northumberland Fusiliers, died on 16th September, 1916. He is commemorated on the Thiepval Memorial, Somme France.

Mossman Wilson, (Private 290502) 9th Battalion, formerly 7th Battalion, Northumberland Fusiliers; was killed in action on the 23rd April, 1917, aged 27. He was the son of the late John and Sarah Ann Wilson (His brother William was also killed). He is commemorated on the Arras Memorial, Pas de Calias, France.

William Wilson, (Pioneer 129074) 'A' Special Company, Royal Engineers was killed in action on the 29th April, 1917. He is buried in the London Rifle Brigade Cemetery.

Martin Young, (Private 59673) 1st/6th Battalion West Yorkshire Regiment (Prince of Wales's Own), was killed in action on the 11th October, 1918. He was the son of George and Ellen Young of Shilbottle. He is buried at Iwuy Communal Cemetery, Nord France, aged 30.

Bryan Broomfield Weightman

Robert G. Weightman

James John Wilson

Mossman Wilson

On Sunday 13th November, 1921 commencing at 3 pm the parish came together in St. James' Church to dedicate the East Window which is the church's war memorial.*

The window was designed by Professor Ronald Hatton. It portrays the suffering of Christ and the names of the fallen which are carved into the pre-existing reredos.

Two plaques which were removed from the walls of what was the War Memorial Institute on Grange Road are now also displayed on the walls of the south transept.

The Memorial service* in 1921 started solemnly with three Psalms: *5* (beginning 'Give ear to my

St. James' Church war memorial window. The names of the fallen can be seen behind the altar carved into the panels of the reredos.

---

* There are other war memorials in the area, one is displayed on the outside wall of the Jubilee hut in Newton on the Moor; and the Green Hut corner has one, which is also a memorial to miners who died in accidents at Shilbottle Colliery
** The details are extracted from Northumberland Archive record EP 77/36 NRO 13167.

Young men who had been newly elevated from the ranks to first officer status, following the deaths of so many trained Captains and higher ranks during the various coerced pushes across 'no man's land.' Henry Stewart is standing on the right. *Author's collection*

words, O Lord, consider my sighing', 23 (beginning 'The Lord is my Shepherd, I shall not be in want,' and 27 (beginning 'The Lord is my light and salvation, in whom shall I fear.)

These readings were followed by readings from *Isaiah* 61 verses 1-3 (The Spirit of the Lord God is upon me ...).

The *Benedictus* (Blessed be the Lord God of Israel: for He hath visited and redeemed his people ...).

There was then a reading from *Revelation* 7 verses 9 to the end (... Salvation belongs to our Lord who sits on the throne ...).

The *National Anthem* was sung, followed by the saying of the *Apostles Creed* and then a long commendation in a single paragraph commending

> the souls of the faithful delivered from the burdens of the flesh ... and the miseries of this sinful world.

An address was delivered by the Archdeacon of Northumberland, the Venerable Blackett-Ord, before the memorial window was unveiled by His Grace the Duke of Northumberland and dedicated by the Archdeacon. The service came to a conclusion with this prayer:

> Eternal Lord God – who holds all souls in life, remember all those, the brave and true, who have died the death of honour.

A bugler played the *Last Post* and *Reveille* before there was a final blessing and dismissal.

Henry Stewart and Harry Donaldson, both young men from Shilbottle, survived the First World War but were tragically killed in separate incidents underground in Shilbottle Colliery when the coal seams in which they were working collapsed. Henry Stewart died on 8th November 1934 and Harry Donaldson on 9th May 1951.

Harry Donaldson

The Second World War

The men from Shilbottle who joined the various 'pals battalions' to go to war in 1914, and during the later recruiting campaigns throughout the First World War, initially thought that the opportunity to quickly overcome the Kaiser's forces and see a bit of life overseas was a fantastic opportunity for adventure, whilst simultaneously escaping from the hard labour of an underground collier. Sadly, the reality proved to be so tragically different.

When the call to arms came at the beginning of the second war, miners were classed as having reserved occupations. Coal was needed for the war effort – the firing of furnaces, the making of steel, the powering of engines and power stations. Nevertheless, young miners joined up and started their training.

Second World War Fatalities

R.W. Anderson (Regrettably, the author has been unable to find details of all fatalities of serving men from the Parish of Shilbottle).

A. Armstrong

Joseph Berry, DFC and 2 Bars, (Squadron Leader, Flying Officer 118435, 501 Squadron Royal Air Force Volunteer Reserve) died on 2nd October, 1944, aged 24 in an air operation over Holland. He was the son of Mr and Mrs J. Berry of 3, Elmfield Terraqce, Hampeth; and husband of Joyce Margaret Berry, of Nottingham. He is buried at Scheemda Protestant Cemetery, Groningen, Netherlands.

Andrew Knox, Corporal 556229, 2nd Battalion Gordon Highlanders, died 16th July 1943, aged 28 while a prisoner of the Japanese. Grandson of William Knox, of Shilbottle. Andrew was buried at Kanchanaburi War Cemetery, Thailand.

J.H. Madden

Kenneth Forrest Middlemist, Warrant Officer (Pilot) 1376378, 112 Squadron, Royal Air Force Volunteer Reserve. He died on 15th September, 1943, aged 23. He was the son of James and Ann Anderson Middlemist of Shilbottle and is buried in Salemo Ware Cemetery.

Andrew Knox

Colliers including Jimmy Lloyd, Thomas Swordy and Mr Hodgson from Longdyke and Shilbottle undertaking training on the Pastures, near Alnwick Castle at the beginning of the Second World War. Midway through their training when it was discovered that most of them were miners some were sent back to Shilbottle Colliery rather than being sent to war.

Families in villages like Shilbottle were, and still are, closely related and have special bonds of association and affection. On the left is the image of Trooper Thomas Swordy. His wife, formerly Margaret Carr, was the youngest sister of Thomas Carr who is shown on the right.

The two men enlisted at Alnwick; Thomas Swordy into Northumberland Hussars, Thomas Carr into the Auxiliary Pioneer Corps. Thomas Carr had lied about his occupation, saying he was a labourer when in fact he worked as a miner at Whittle. He was among the 300,000 soldiers on the beaches of Dunkirk in 1940 who were retreating from the advancing Germans. Not long before this retreat, he sent the post card message shown below to his sister Margaret, Thomas Swordy's sister.

On the 17th June 1940, Thomas Carr was one of the servicemen taken in small vessels to be boarded onto the H.M.T. *Lancastria*, a requisitioned Cunard liner. Four miles off Saint-Nazaire the liner received three direct hits from a German Junker 88 Bomber. Within 20 minutes the liner sank taking with her an estimated 4,000 men including Thomas Carr.

At home in Alnwick 36 year old Thomas Carr had a young wife, a son and two daughters. His second son Thomas was born nine days after his father was reported missing and later confirmed dead.

Thomas is buried in Pornic Military Cemetery (*below*) on the south side of the Loire Estuary.

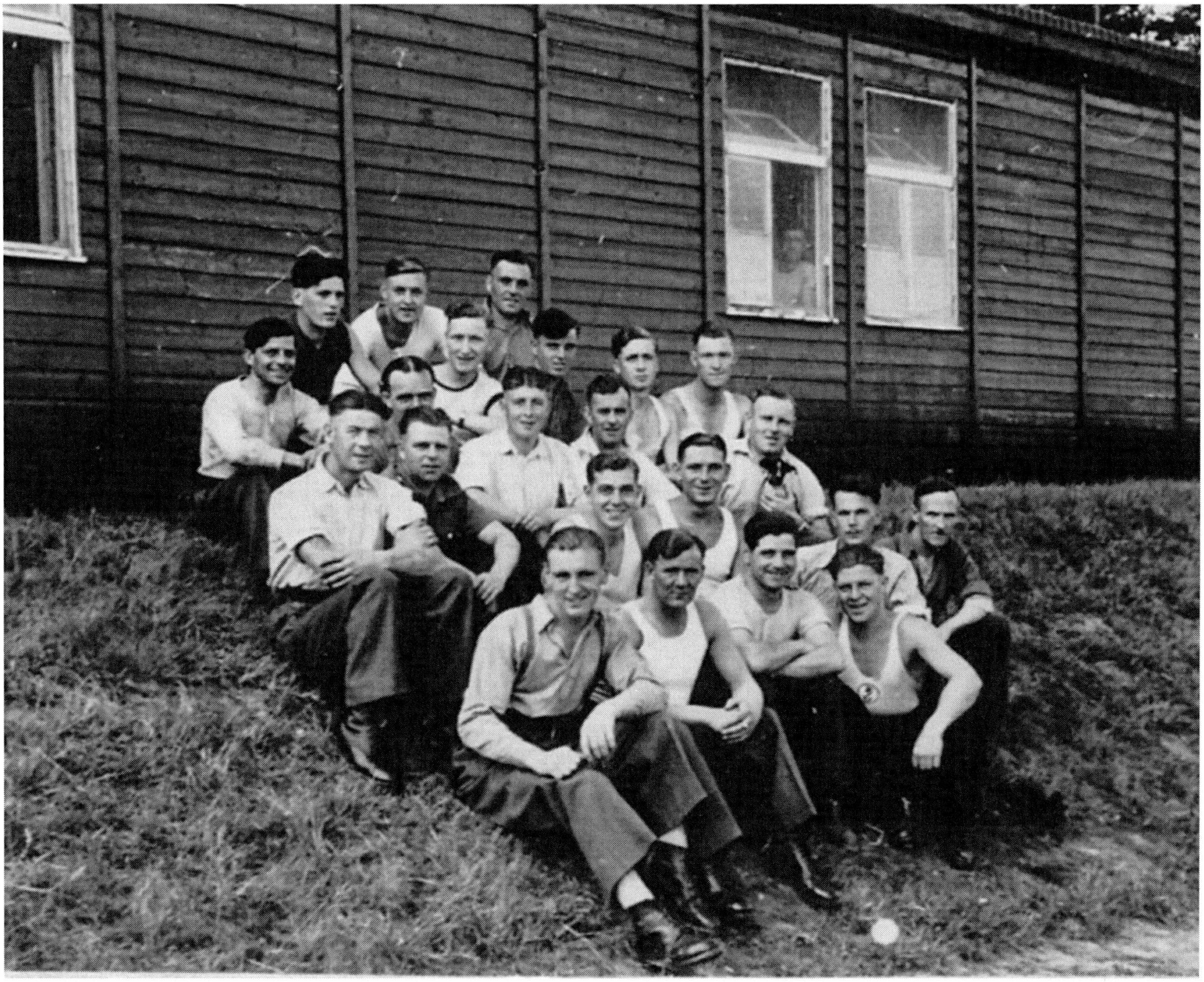

Thomas Carr's brother David sitting at the front of the picture with Shilbottle and Alnwick lads as prisoners of war at Blachhimmla, Heydebreck, Germany. They were also on the beaches of Dunkirk before being captured.

Julia Tweedy collection

Kriegsgefangenenpost

Postkarte

PASSED P.W.4118

An Mrs M. Carr C/o Mr T. Swordy
No 7 Percy Rd Shilbottle

Gebührenfrei!

Absender:

Vor- und Zuname: David Carr

Gefangenennummer: 5817

Feldpost-Nr. 27 340 A

Deutschland (Allemagne)

Empfangsort: Alnwick

Straße: Northumberland

Land: England

Landesteil (Provinz usw.)

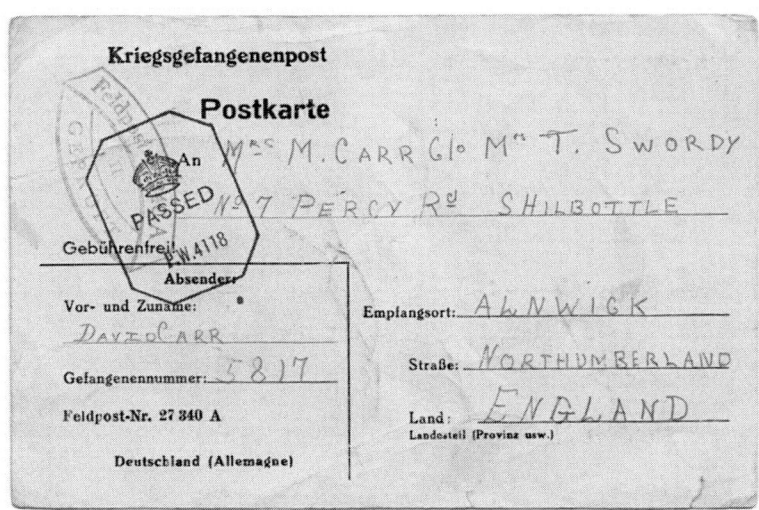

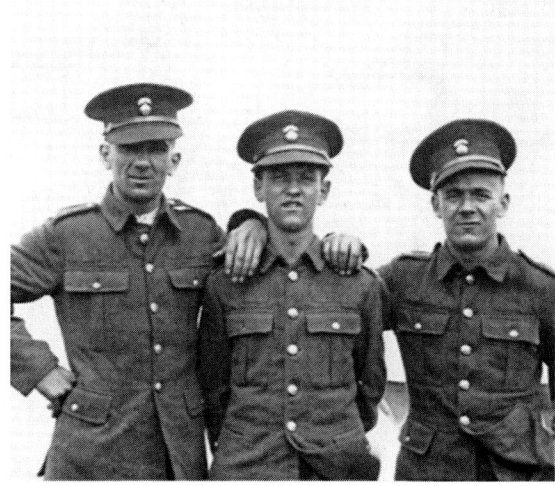

Between 21st January and 2nd February 1945 257,000 Western Allies prisoners of war were forcibly marched hundreds of miles to PoW camps in Poland. Many of the men on the Long March did not survive. David Carr is on the right of the photograph above and his postcard home via 7 Percy Road, Shilbottle.

Julia Tweedy collection

G. Porteous

John Thomas Pringle, Stoker First Class, C/KX 96537, H.M.S. Juno, Royal Navy. He died on 21st May 1941 aged 23. He was the son of Robert Antony and Margaret Pringle, and husband of Annie Tait Pringle of Shilbottle. He is commemorated at Chatham Naval Memorial. The HMS Juno, J Class Destroyer was sunk by Italian aircraft in the Mediterranean.

Dennis Simm, Corporal 611943, Royal Air Force, died on the 18th February, 1945 aged 24. He was the son of John and Margaret Simm of Shilbottle. He is buried in Alnwick Cemetery.

Jowsey Richardson Straughan, Aircraftman 1st class 1503294, Royal Air Force Volunteer Reserve, died on 27th February, 1944 aged 22. He was the son of Joseph and Elizabeth Straughan of Shilbottle and is buried in Calcutta (Bhowanipore) Cemetery, Kolkata, India.

S. Thompson.

John Ian Truman, Driver 2090542, Royal Engineers, died on 3rd September, 1946 aged 28. He was the son of Mark and Isabella A. Truman and is buried in St. James Churchyard, Shilbottle.

Percival William Weightman, Sergeant 533027, 224 Squadron, Royal Air Force, died on 21st June, 1940 aged 22. He was the son of Robert William and Frances Edith Weightman of Shilbottle. Sergeant Weightman's Lockheed Hudson aircraft of Coastal Command, with three other crew members, failed to return from convoy escort duties in the North Sea. He is commemorated at Runnymede Memorial, Surrey.

Edward Anthony Fitzherbert Widdrington M.C., 5th Royal Enniskillen Dragoon Guards, Royal Armoured Corps and 2nd Special Air Service Regiment, Army Air Corps., died on 20th January 1944 aged 29 years. He also served with the Transjordan Frontier Force. He was the son of Brigadier-General Betram Fitzherbert Widdrington, C.M.G., D.S.O., and Enid Widdrington of Newton on the Moor, Felton. He is commemorated at the Assisi War Cemetery.

Support From Home

Parents, relatives and children of those serving overseas knitted socks, wrote letters of support and contributed to parcels of food as they waited prayerfully for news of their loved ones. Above is the Empire Day Certificate from the King sent to Julia Tweedy (née Swordy) acknowledging her support.

Aden (South Arabia, 1966)

Robert Jeffrey Hughes, Gunner 23994669, B. Battery, 1st Regiment Royal Horse Artillery, died 28th April 1966, aged 18. He was one of three men killed and three wounded during a 105mm rocket attack by dissident tribesmen on Monke Field Camp, Radfan. The two other men killed were Sergeant 23547142 Brian Dunkley aged 26, and Gunner 23978525 Silas Bartley aged 21.

The Village's War and Mineworkers' Memorial.

The village's war memorial and memorial to miner's killed in Shilbottle collieries is a few yards east of St. James' Church, on the corner where the Green Hut had been located.

Crashed Spitfire

During the latter stages of the Second World War, the airfield at Eshott, a few miles south of Shilbottle, was used for the training of Spitfire pilots. On 7th May, 1943, following a mid-air collision with another aircraft, Spitfire registration P8144 crashed in a field a few yards north-east of Colliers' Close, Shilbottle. The pilot was not seriously injured and was helped from the aeroplane by villager, Mr Charles (Chuck) Prentice. The Spitfire was damaged beyond repair.

A tragic drowning

On 17th January, 1945, only a few weeks before the end of the Second World War, ten young soldiers on a training exercise at Guyzance were swept to their deaths during a river-crossing exercise. Against the advice of locals who knew the dangers of the river when in flood the young men, who were fully equipped with heavy weapons, armaments and clothing, entered the River Coquet a mile upriver from the old iron works' weir and were swept downstream, where their craft overturned at the weir head. They were unable to save themselves and were drowned.

The men were Lance Corporal M. Fredlieb and Private N. Ashton of the Duke of Wellington Regiment and Privates P.G. Clements, E. King, K. Lee, A. Leighton, M.M. Feddelty, J.W. Wilson, R.H.B. Winteringham and A. Yates, all of the Durham Light Infantry. All were 18 years of age.

A memorial marking the site of the tragedy, where the young men lost their lives, stands on the north bank of the River Coquet at Guyzance.

Shilbottle's Prominent People

It will be clear from the preceding pages that there have been some very able people raised in the village, people who never sought public acclaim, who in their own way achieved greatness of a humble, unassuming nature. Mention has been made of miners possessed of great intelligence and potential who of necessity left school at fourteen to help support their families. Young women too whose employment opportunities were limited to the village or nearby town.

Readers will have noted in the text the names of families whose lineage goes back generations. They will be aware of boys who moved through colliery ranks as men to hold management positions; and women who provided the energy to drive forward social and community enterprises. Often the same people, their siblings or offspring, are mentioned because they represented the village at sport, team management, local politics, community or religious activities. Some people from humble origins, with hardly any expectations, have been included in this chapter because they went on to become leaders in and beyond the village.

It is acknowledged, however, that this chapter fails to do justice to the many people who deserve a mention; lads who went on to own their own removal business; those who had highly regarded building and scaffolding companies; some who left the village and carved out successful careers as police officers, nurses, teachers and civil servants. Space, failure to identify them, or the individuals' reluctance to be named, has reduced this final section to a select few; those people who have been honoured nationally and some very obvious people who have distinguished themselves in their careers or through visible public service.

Below are a few of the people who have contributed to the life of the village of Shilbottle, or who came from the village and made their mark beyond it.

Sir John Robinson Felton K.B.E.

Sir John Robinson Felton K.B.E.

John Felton lived in Shilbottle between 1880 and 1891 and completed some of his early education at Shilbottle's Church of England School. He went on to study at King's College, Newcastle (then part of the University of Durham) before serving his apprenticeship as a mining engineer at West Stanley Colliery and at Stobswood. He became the certificated Colliery Manager of West Stanley in 1903.

In 1908, he became Assistant Inspector of Mines for South Staffordshire, and from 1915 Senior Mines Inspector for Yorkshire and the North Midland Division. In 1924 he was elevated to Divisional Inspector. Between 1942 and 1947 he was Deputy Chief Inspector of Mines and then His Majesty's Chief Inspector of Mines, based at the Ministry of Fuel and Power. In 1920 Mr Felton was appointed O.B.E. and in 1946 he was knighted. The then vicar of Shilbottle, the Reverend William Hume, wrote to him on behalf of the Church School and Parish to congratulate him. Sir John Robinson Felton responded: *I cannot but feel grateful for all the help of the school and church in those formative years.*

The Revd Percy Lee

The Reverend Percy Lee

Percy Lee was born in 1863 in Brampton. His University education was at Hertford College, Oxford. He was ordained by Bishop Wilberforce (son of the slave abolitionist) in Newcastle Cathedral in 1886 and became curate at Warkworth. Lee married Emily, his training vicar's daughter. He served as vicar at Birtley (near Chollerford) before coming to Shilbottle in November 1900. While vicar of Shilbottle he encouraged the founding of groups for people of all ages: sporting, educational and spiritual. When a large proportion of the community's men signed up and went off to war from 1914 – some never to return – Lee held a service every weekday during which the soldiers were prayed for by name. He set up a shrine to the memory of the fallen at the water-pant on North Side and he held open-air services of remembrance there and in St. James' Church. He initiated a Comforts Fund to support those away and commissioned the village war memorial consisting of a stained-glass window to go above the altar in church, with the names of the fallen carved into the ornamental reredos screen beneath it.

Lee and his wife Emily (who died in 1918) recruited and trained a number of volunteer lady church-workers in Newton and Shilbottle.

As a result of Act of Parliament, Parochial Church Councils were established by 1920 and Shilbottle's P.C.C. met for the first time just a few months before Lee resigned. This was after twenty years in the parish. In retirement, with Ellen his second wife, he moved to Alnwick. Sadly, Ellen died in 1926 but Percy Lee busied himself, helping out local parishes and chairing

Alnwick Rural District Council and Alnwick Board of Guardians until shortly before his death in 1948.

When building work began for Lee Avenue, in Shilbottle the Parish Council recommended that *because of the substantial contribution to the life of the local community Reverend Lee had made*, the former vicar's surname be used for the estate.

Peter Leatherland

Peter Leatherland

Peter Leatherland was born in Newport in 1928. He was raised in Gloucester. Aged 14 he joined the Merchant Navy before enlisting in the Royal Navy as a weapons rating. When his age was discovered he left the Navy and began work as a collier, first of all at Gilsland before moving across to the King Pit at Haltwhistle. He came to Shilbottle in 1949 to work as a face-worker at the Grange Pit. He soon got involved in union work and was elected the colliery's National Union of Mineworkers' Secretary, a position he held until 1969. He was sent to America by the National Coal Board to lecture about British mining techniques. For many years Peter was also a village councillor. In this role he was instrumental in negotiating improvements for retired miners and in particular their living accommodation. He was badly injured in the colliery and left the mining industry to train as a teacher at Alnwick Training College in 1969. He qualified in 1971 and went to work at Gallowhill Special School near Whalton outside of Morpeth. In recognition of his contribution to the village of Shilbottle the Village Council agreed in 1961 that the Aged Miners' Cottages near St. James' Church should be renamed in his honour as Leatherland Road. Peter died on 6th January 2003.

Christopher Lendrum C.B.E., Hon D.Litt.

Christopher Lendrum has been one of four churchwardens at St. James' Shilbottle since 2013. He was educated at Durham University, where he met his wife Margaret. After graduating, he was recruited by Barclays

Christopher Lendrum C.B.E.

Bank where he went on to lead the bank's retail and corporate banking divisions with responsibility for all banking affairs in Africa and corporate social responsibility across the world. He retired after 36 years service and lives within the Parish boundaries. He was a national trustee for Citizens' Advice Bureau; a Director of Motability, and of the County Durham, Tyne and Wear and Northumberland Community Foundations. He is involved in a company providing seed-corn money for North East business ventures and he manages a trust in his name which disburses money for needy causes in Shilbottle. He was honoured as Commander of the British Empire in 2005.

Joseph (Joe) Ternent, B.E.M. (1918 – 1995)

Joseph Ternent, B.E.M.

Mr Joe Ternent was born in Alnwick and moved with his family to Shilbottle aged 3. As a young man he took an interest in youth activities in Shilbottle and for many years was a football referee. He was President of Alnwick Bowling Club, was secretary for many years and he represented Northumberland as a bowler.

He was Secretary of Shilbottle's Mine Workers' Union and was a parish councillor before representing Shilbottle on Alnwick Rural District Council, during which time he chaired various committees. He was a Justice of the Peace for 22 years before retiring aged 70. He received the British Empire Medal for his Union and parish community work in 1971 and served on A.R.D.C. until local government was reorganised in 1974.

Mr Tom Robson, Clerk to Alnwick R.D.C. spoke of Joe Ternent as being *a councillor who had his own ideas which he put forward skilfully ... an old type of miner who had lots of common sense*. Former Shilbottle councillor, Mr Ernie Tully said of him that *if you wanted something done Joe Ternent would make it happen*.

Thanks to his daughter Maureen Davis for the biography and photograph

Mrs Maria Elisabeth Haddow, M.B.E.

Elisabeth Haddow moved to Shilbottle in 1987 when her husband bought the village post office. When she retired from her head teacher's post at Red Row First School in 1997 she was drawn into the Village Forum

Mrs Maria Elisabeth Haddow, M.B.E. (*right*) receiving her M.B.E. from the Duchess of Northumberland

Lilian Hume

and later the combined Shilbottle and Hampeth Social Organisation, of which she became chair. One of the Organisation's first ventures was a village gala, financed through the National Lottery. Hundreds of villagers turned out to support the event which ended in a veterans' football match between the vicar and postmaster's teams. Thereafter, the post office became the centre for money making ventures, which led to planters being built for flowers across the parish, a village Co-operative being developed, play areas being refurbished in the village and a new one being established at Hampeth. In 2002 Elisabeth became a parish councillor and a district councillor where at that level she became chair of policy scrutiny for the District, and chair of Alnwick District Health Forum. This was while she was also working with members of the combined Social Organisation to access funding for a new village hall. After 10 years the Big Lottery granted £450,000 towards the 1 million pound costs. The new hall opened in August 2010. That year in recognition her work for the regeneration of Shilbottle, Elisabeth was awarded an M.B.E., which was presented by the Lord Lieutenant and Duchess of Northumberland at Alnwick Castle in the presence of many of the people who helped in the regeneration and funding process for Shilbottle.

Lilian Hume

Lilian was born in Shilbottle and started playing the piano for St. James' Sunday School as a youngster. As a teenager she took organ lesson with Reverend Jackson at Lesbury and in 1945 she was the established as organist at her village church in Shilbottle. During her 75 years to date as organist Lilian has been instrumental in organising Nativity Plays, pantomimes and other theatrical and musical events across the parish. For 30 years she was also one of the church wardens at St. James' Church. In addition to her church work, she has played a pivotal role in the village's Women's Institute, the Girls Guild, Mothers' Union and Over 60s Club. She taught embroidery to ladies in Alnwick for many years and ran a craft group in Acklington Prison. On 4th May 2012, on the date of Her Majesty the Queen's Diamond Jubilee, she was one of 86 men and 86 women from across the nation to receive Maundy Money from the Queen at York Minster. The Diocesan bishop at that time, the Right Reverend Martin Wharton, said of Lilian that

> she had an outstanding record of service, dedication and faithfulness to the life of the community of Shilbottle, expressed through her long involvement in her parish church.'

Reverend Patricia Elinor Rennison (née Swordy)

Reverend Patricia Elinor Rennison

Pat Rennison was born in Shilbottle, educated at the village school then Amble Secondary Modern School, where she later worked as a laboratory assistant. She was a Sunday School teacher at St. James' Church in the village until she was married and was church warden between 1994 and 2002. She was licensed as a reader in the parish in 2001 and ordained deacon as a local minister in Shilbottle in 2011. She was ordained priest in 2012. In addition to her church activities, funerals, services and pastoral visiting, she has helped with the Amicale French connection, the annual flower show and the various social and fund raising activities connected with the old people's trips and treats.

Shilbottle's Prominent People

Thomas William Scott.

Thomas William Scott.

Thomas William Scott came into Shilbottle village from Burradon on Tyneside in the 1960s. In January 1970, Tommy was elected as a parish councillor for Shilbottle. He was 36 years old then and worked in Shilbottle Colliery as a face-worker. On the retirement of Mr Peter Leatherland he became chairman of the Shilbottle Branch of the Mineworkers' Union and susbequently chairman of the council, chairman of the working men's club and chairman of the Shilbottle Miners' Recreation Ground Charity. As chairman of the parish council, a postition he has held for over 30 years, he has worked alongside three parish clerks and many councillors. Throughout he has remained dedicated to the community of Shilbottle, working for and supporting many changes in the village. He has overseen the opening of the Community Hall, the building of flower planters and the placing of new seats around the village. He was instrumental in securing extensions to cemeteries in the village, the creation of new play areas for children, the establishment of a Memorial Garden for the Mining Community and in 2014 the erection of the War Memorial at Green Hut Corner.

As an 87 year old, Tommy continues to be an active chair of the parish council.

On 6th November 2019 the Shilbottle Parish Council bestowed on Tommy the title of **Honorary Freeman of the Village of Shilbottle**. This was in recognition of his outstanding and dedicated commitment to the community of Shilbottle for the past 50 years, an honour which is only bestowed in rare and exceptional circumstances, and as such, was the first time the village of Shilbottle had granted the award of Honorary Freeman.

Robert Whitehead

Robert Whitehead

With his father's encouragement, Robert started playing the Accordion as a 10 year old. He took lessons from local man Jack McManus, an excellent piano player. His brother John was learning to play the drums and as the 'Whitehead Brothers' they played their first gig at St. James' Church Garden fete in 1963. The Whitehead duo was joined by pianist Alan Brown and they played at charity events across North Northumberland and later in County Durham. In 1969 the band was extended with a fiddle player and bass player. That year they appeared on *Opportunity Knocks*.

With a name change to 'Danelaw Dance Band' the group played Ceilidh music, their biggest performance being at Newcastle's Mayfair Ballroom, playing for 800 Irish dancers. Branching into the Scottish country dance scene they began to travel the country. Robert competed as a soloist winning many high placings in competitive events. In 1968 he was the first accordionist from south of the Border to win the All Scottish Championship. The Danelaws played on Radio Newcastle's Barn Dance series in the early 1970s and in 1978 they were the first band from England to play on BBC Scotland's *Take the Floor* programme. He and his band have played regularly at the Shetland Accordion and Fiddle Festival and they have represented 'Scotland' at the Smithsonian Folk Life Festival in Washington DC. Robert has been honoured by the Association of Accordion and Fiddle Clubs. In 2015 he and his band were invited to play for the Caledonian Society of Uganda at their Ex-pats St Andrew's Ball. They also played for 800 male inmates of Kampala Jail for a Ceilidh. After 55 years his band continues to play, albeit with slightly different personnel, however the original pianist remains as does drummer of 30 years. His youngest son Graeme Whitehead now also plays the accordion with the Danelaws. Robert recalls his first music teacher asking him if he 'knew what he was taking on?' His answer now is 'hours of enjoyment.'

Mr Kenneth Willcox M.B.E.

Kenneth Willcox was born in Shilbottle, married in Shilbottle and raised two sons and two daughters in the village. He started work at Shilbottle Colliery as a fifteen year old and retired, through injury, from the colliery just before it closed in 1982. For over 50 years Kenneth Willcox worked tirelessly raising funds for Shilbottle football teams. Through weekly bingo sessions during that time he raised thousands of pounds to pay for outings for the village's 'Old Folk'. He won the village's small garden competition many years running. In 2006, aged 77 he received an M.B.E. from Her Majesty the Queen at Buckingham Palace.

Mr Kenneth Willcox receiving his M.B.E. from Queen Elizabeth II

Mr Keith Wilson, MSc., CEng, MIMechE, FIMMM.

Keith Wilson was born in Shilbottle and attended the Council School in the village. Aged 11 he went to Amble County Secondary Modern School, leaving with a handful of G.C.Es. Aged 16 he found work at Hill Porter's in Alnwick as a trainee draughtsman before beginning a Craft Apprenticeship at Shilbottle Colliery. While attending the Mining School at Ashington he was offered a student engineering apprenticeship which lasted five years and included working as site engineer for the construction of the blending plant at Alcan's Aluminium smelting works at Lynemouth. On the completion of his apprenticeship he was appointed deputy engineer at Lynemouth Colliery before being appointed to the Engineer's post at Backworth Colliery. From there he was appointed Group Engineer for the collieries of Ellington, Lynemouth and Ashington. During this period, through part-time study at Newcastle Polytechnic, he added a Master of Science degree in engineering, science and technology to his professional qualification of Chartered Engineer. In 1982 he was appointed British Coal Corporation's Head of Engineering for the North East Region. In this position he had the supervision of 400 chief engineers and 3,000 mechanics and engineers. In 1989 he left British Coal to take up the post of technical director for the Young Mining Group and spent some time in Venezuela. After leaving Young's in 1993 he created his own independent management consultancy. His clients included Thames Water, Young Group plc. Banks Group and British Coal. In 1994 he was recruited by Banks Group as operational director and head of mining, a position he held until 1999. In April of that year he became director of engineering for the Port of Tyne and three years later chief executive and managing director until his retirement in 2008.

Mr Keith Wilson,

ABOUT THE AUTHOR

Barry Stewart B.A., D.M.S., M.Phil., (Social Policy), M.Phil., (Theology), retired from Northumbria Police in 1994 in the rank of Detective Chief Superintendent. For 10 years thereafter he was the Social Responsibility Adviser in the Diocese of Newcastle.

SHILBOTTLE – its past and its people is Barry Stewart's third local history book. His others also published by Stenlake Publishing Limited are *BILTON BANKS – The Pit and Its People*, and *CRAMLINGTON its past and its people*. He has also published two crime novels, both of which are available as electronic books on Amazon, and a small book of humorous poems the profits from which were donated to The Sir Bobby Robson cancer Foundation.

Front cover upper: Percy Road and St. James Church, Shilbottle *lower:* Shilbottle Grange Colliery.   *Keith Wilson collection*
Back cover: A group of lads at the beginning of the 1920s doing a spot of gardening at the Church of England School under the supervision of Mr Carr.   *Keith Wilson collection*